40 Methods every Innovation Manager must know!

Contents

Summary

The book lists a variety of proven tools for innovation management. The methods can be applied in different aspects of innovation including processes, solving problems, enhancing creativity, and Leadership. They also support the definition of strategy, decision making and evaluation. Furthermore it refers to a number of methods such a TRIZ, lean innovation and others.

Introduction

In changing positions, roles and companies, I have worked on the topic of "innovation" for many years. For me it remains thrilling and exiting but despite many experiences, I always keep on learning new things.

In this book, I have collected some of the most interesting and (for me) relevant methods that help to manage, foster, improve, tackle or operationalize innovation. It is a compendium, **not** a detailed description. I have included many references for those interested in further information. As it is a very dynamic topic, I don`t aim to provide a complete collection of methods. Nevertheless, I would like to provide some personally tested tools for daily work.

Innovation Strategy

Innovation is strategic for many companies. This chapter shall give an overview of some relevant methods for the development of strategies. It shall not replace a strategy textbook. Nevertheless, some of the most useful tools are listed.

Macro Environment (PESTEL)

The following analysis method gives information on the macro environment and drivers of change in the described market by researching relevant data for the political, economic, social, technological, environmental and legal situation of a market. It is often used to analyse the market potential of an innovation and is a foundation for further strategy development (See fig. 1).

Political	o (E.g.) In 2010, total healthcare spending in China reached 164 Billion $ and expected to grow at a CAGR of 19% through 2015 to reach about 410 Billion USD. o The healthcare market in China is expected to continue to grow dramatically, in part, due to the government's 125 Billion USD package spent during the period 2009-12. o …
Economic	o (e.g.)The average disposable income of urban household in China is expected to increase to 8,383 USD by 2025. o The unemployment rate in China is expected remain at 4% over the next few years. o Inflation is expected to remain stable at 3% over the next decade. o …
Social	o The total population in China is expected to shrink by 0.08 percent by 2050, from 1.4 billion in 2010 to 1.3 billion in 2050. o Cancer incidence is expected to increase by more than 200 percent between 2010 and 2030, from 2.6 million to 6.3 million.
Technology	o Gross domestic R & D spending exceeded 140 billion USD in 2010 in China. The R&D spend accounted for a share of 1.5% of GDP.
Environmental	o The various effects of climate change pose risks on public health in China. o To protect human health and environment against various pollutants and hazardous materials, the Chinese government has developed various rules and regulations that span across many environmental categories.
Legal	o State Food and Drug Administration is the legal authority responsible for Drugs, Medical Devices and Biological Products. [1]

Figure 1: PESTEL analysis (data for illustration only).

---

[1] See Cheers Interactive India (2011), p. 3.

SWOT

An analysis of strengths, weaknesses, opportunities and threats is useful to gain insight into the situation of a company. It is a commonly used and described tool. In innovation, it can be used to analyse the innovation internal core competencies or deficits of a company. Opportunities and threats can be used to evaluate new external business opportunities or threats by new innovative competitors. It is a very important tool when communicating to managers (see (fig. 2).

Strengths	Weaknesses
• E.g. Clear strategic focus on profitability instead of market share (dropping non-profitable customers) • High quality customer base	• Still low reputation
Opportunities	**Threats**
• Invest in fast growing segment (M&A) • Further expand high-value segment • Continue growth momentum in current business	• Intense focus on profitability erodes market share and creates a gap in the portfolio that might hinder sustainable growth • Loss of key employees due to internal uncertainty

Figure 2: SWOT analysis. Content for illustration only.

Industrial Analysis

The analysis of the competitive situation in a target market is a pertinent task.[2] In combination with the analysis of the internal environment, it gives a baseline for the design of a strategy. After a sound analysis of the target market and its opportunities, a suitable offering can be found or designed.

A well-known model for analysing a targeted industry in order to craft a strategy is the five forces model of competition by Porter. The model analyses *"(1) competition from rival sellers, (2) competition from potential new entrants to the industry, (3) competition from producers of substitute products, (4) supplier bargaining power, and (5) customer bargaining power."*[3]

Five competitive forces can hurt prospective profits:

- Customers can force down prices if their bargaining power is high enough.

- Powerful suppliers may constrain profits if they are able to enforce higher prices.

- Aspiring entrants, armed with new capacity, can ratchet up the investment required for a company to stay in the game.

- Rivals can force down prices or increase quality for the same price.

- Substitute offerings can lure customers away.[4]

Recent literature extends the model with other aspects such as the impact of the cooperation between companies and the macro environment.

---

[2] See Thompson, A.A. et al. (2012), p. 97.
[3] Thompson, A.A. et al. (2012), p. 102.
[4] See Porter; M. (2008), p.79 pp.

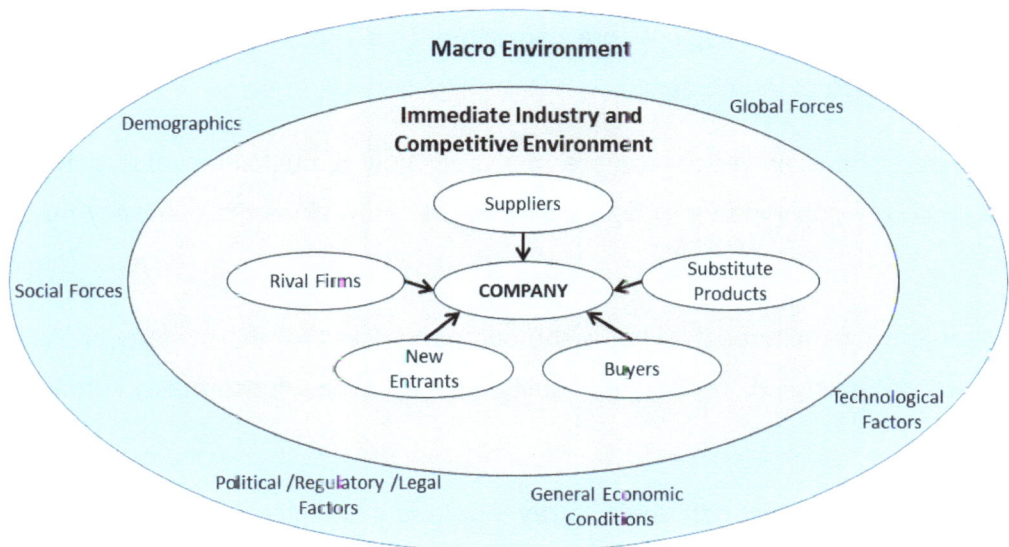

Figure 3: Porters Five Forces embedded into Macro Environment[5]

The macro environment contains different influencing factors as the general economic conditions, demographics, global forces, social forces and technological developments, political-, legal and regulatory factors which can change the market dramatically. Examples are changes in laws which can restrict or prohibit a newly developed product. The model can be used to analyse the intensity of competition, to work out drivers of change and to spot attractive niches where competition is still low (see fig. 3).[6]

Strategy Mapping

In some cases it is unclear what the current strategy of a company is. In such cases, it is necessary to analyze the different elements and actions of the company and derive its growth perspective, its main processes, customer advantages and financial potential.

---

[5] See Thompson, A.A. et al. (2012), p. 99.
[6] See Thompson, A.A. et al. (2012), p. 119.

In a first step, the attitude of the employees and the predominant culture is captured. Furthermore, the main technological core competences are gathered to gain insight on the growth perspective of the company.

In a second step, the main processes are analyzed: how is customer value achieved? How is the company positioned in process excellence? How does the company manage innovation?

The customer is a crucial aspect. What is the company doing for the customer? What is the customer receiving in terms of quality, price, time, functionality, image or relationship?

Last, all these activities must contribute to revenue and productivity, which results in an increased shareholder value.

These steps can be used to proof the strategy of the own company for consistency or to analyze competitors (see fig 4.).

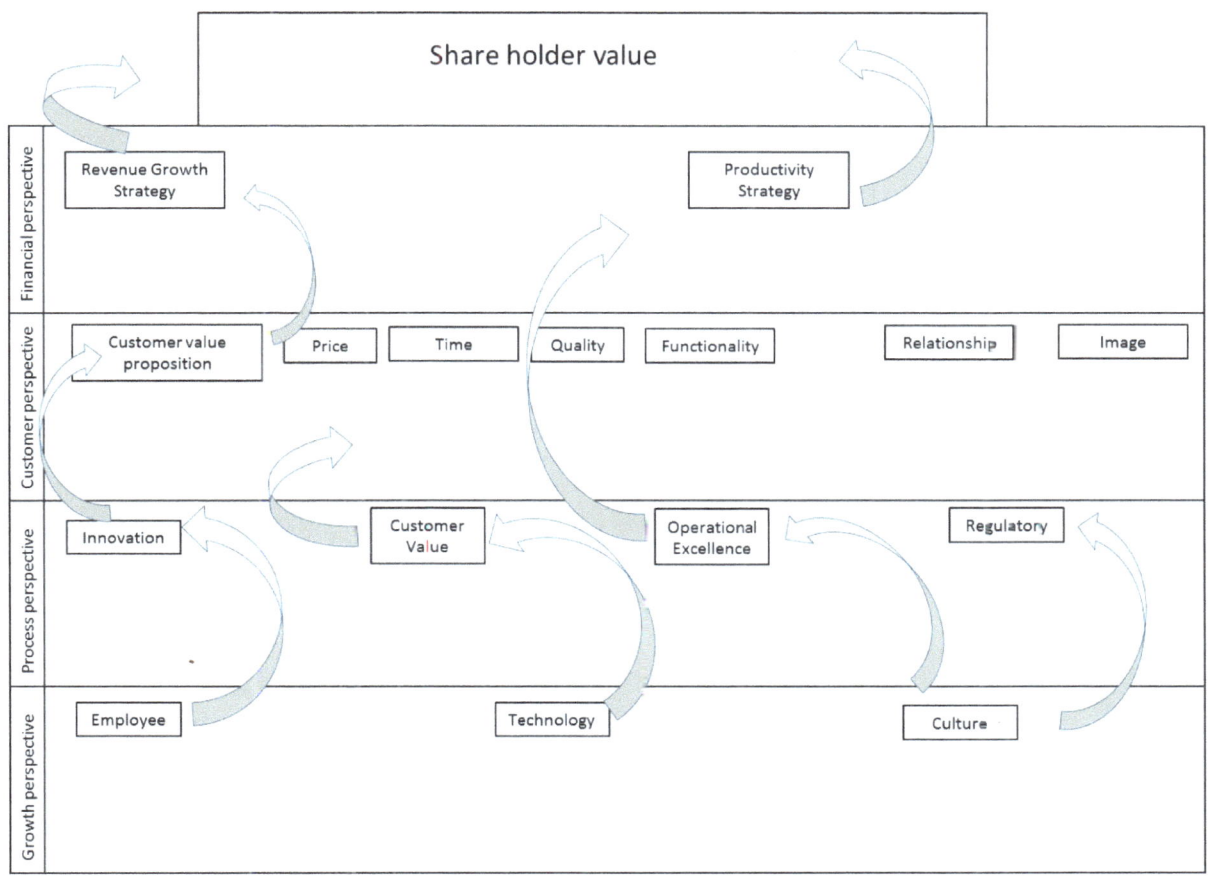

Figure 4: Strategy mapping.

Balanced Score Card

A Balanced Scorecard is a well-used tool for strategy implementation. It is a set of measures and actions (and related key performance indicators) in the areas of processes, finance (and human resources), customer and innovation. The actions in those areas strive to achieve a vision. A vision is a strong image of the future like e.g. the statement by John F. Kennedy of "bringing a man to the moon and back home safely by the end of the decade".

To achieve this vision, new processes in development are required, funding must be available and new technologies need to be developed. Within the dimension of processes, finance, innovation and customer, measures must be taken. The outcome of these measures is frequently observed and key performance indicators are reported to the management. This tool is helpful to formulate concrete tasks and projects to achieve specific strategic objectives (see fig. 5). [7]

As considerable resources are deployed into R&D and innovation but the results are obtained far in the future, it is important to monitor outcomes.[8] The Balanced Scorecard is a strategic measurement and control system that uses both financial and non-financial measures adopted by practitioners to define and measure the performance of an organization.[9] It is a proven method for the business. It's use in R&D organizations, however, is relatively new.[10]

In "real live" there might be some skepticism towards Balanced Scorecards. Scientists and engineers are not necessarily averse to performance measurement. They are skeptical of and averse to the idea of "measuring for the sake of measuring only" without any real and meaningful effect on research output or performance.[11] For this reason, a set of reasonable indicators must be found, ideally together with the researchers and innovators.

---

[7] See Kaplan, R.S. et al. (2005), n.p.
[8] See Jyoti, D.K.B. et al. (2006), p. 879.
[9] See Jyoti, D.K.B. et al. (2006), p. 879.
[10] See Osama, A. (2006), p. 7–9.
[11] See Osama, A. (2006),P.227.

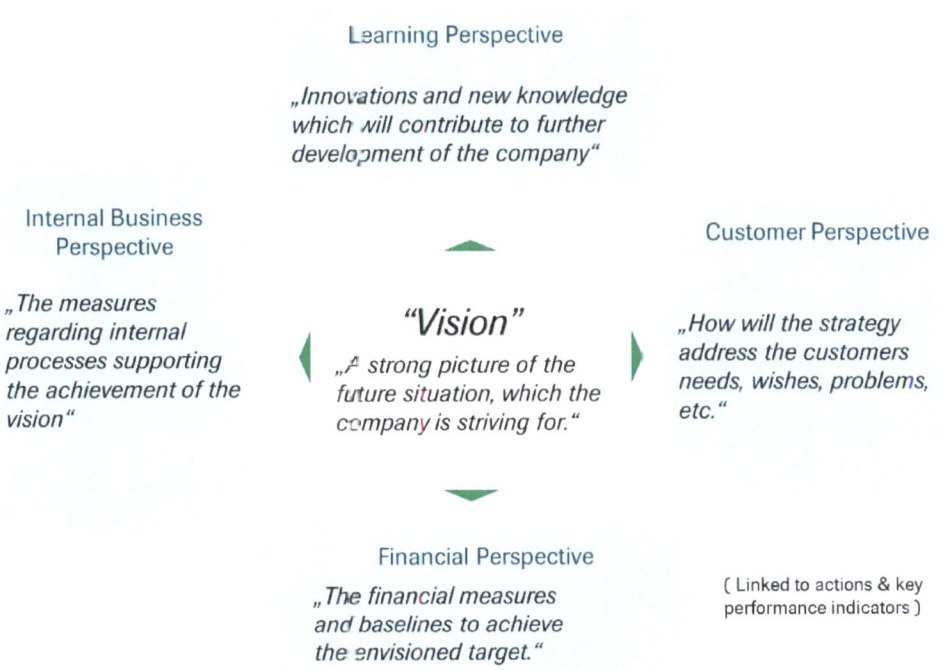

Figure 5: Balanced Scorecard.

Key Performance Indicators

Key performance indicators (KPI) can measure the status quo of important processes, critical projects or the organization. They are used to control, to improve or to steer the organization and to monitor the fulfillment of strategic goals. They must be linked to strategic goals as described above within e.g. a balanced score card approach.

Obtaining KPIs can require considerable effort as systems must be implemented and the organization must be convinced to provide this information. Especially, in R&D and innovation, KPIs are often criticized as they do not provide the same accuracy as in e.g. shop floor management. Nevertheless, it is important to highlight the strategic goals of the organization and the KPI as indicator if the organization is on track. In some cases it might be enough to use qualitative indicators.

Some examples of Innovation KPIs:

KPI
No. of new ideas
No. of high quality patents
No. of open innovation ideas
No. of projects related to new ideas
No. of publications

Figure 6: Examples of Key Performance Indicators (KPI).

Competitive Advantage

For each business, there are several critical success factors, which can be collected by interviewing experienced marketers or managers. Fig. 7 lists some example success factors and their rating of importance collected during an interview. During the same interview these factors can be rated for the main competitors in this market. The results can be presented as in fig. 8. The results can give interesting insights were your company has strengths or weaknesses. The results can also be used e.g. to foster innovations in areas of specific strength or look for partner who can balance certain weaknesses.

Success Factors	Rating of Importance
Performance	1
Flexibility	1
Reliability of product	2
Service	2
Cost	2

Figure 7: Critical success factors obtained from interview (examples).

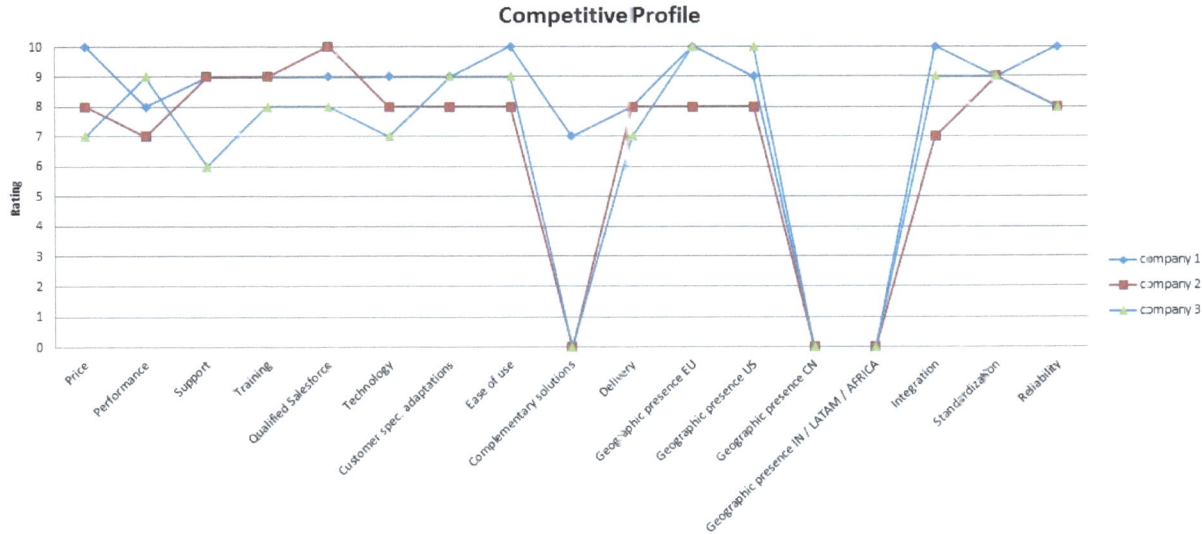

Figure 8: Competitive profile of 3 companies.

Blue Ocean

The Blue Ocean Strategy approach is based on the idea to create a new unoccupied market space without any direct competition to avoid the so-called bloody "Red Ocean". A Blue Ocean is created in an area where a company's actions favourably affect both its cost structure and its value proposition to buyers. Cost savings are made from eliminating and reducing the factors an industry competes on, e.g. elimination of distribution chain by online sales platforms.

Buyer value is lifted by raising and creating elements the industry has never offered. Over time, costs are reduced further as scale economies kick in, due to the high sales volumes that superior value generates (see figure 9.).[12] The most important tool to identify such unoccupied market spaces is the Buyer Utility Map (next chapter).

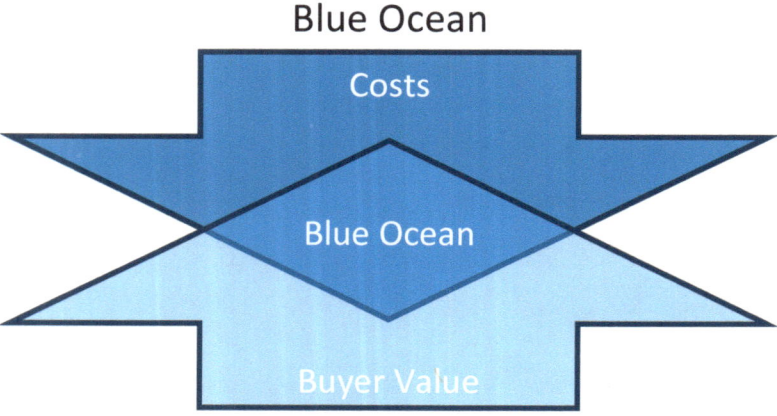

Blue Ocean

Figure 9: Blue Ocean strategy principle.[13]

Buyer Utility Map

To achieve the so called "Blue Ocean Strategy" the right levers of utility for customers must be identified. Buyer value is increased by raising and creating elements the industry has never offered.

The Buyer Utility Map helps managers to focus on the customer utility. The application of the Buyer Utility Map helps to identify new market spaces within the business and allow a new positioning of the products in the future. It outlines all the levers companies can

---

[12] See Kim et al. (2004): p.8.
[13] See Kim et al. (2004): p.7.

pull to deliver a useful product or service to customers as well as the different experiences customers can have of a product or service. It enables the identification of the full range of utility propositions that a product or service can offer.[14] It describes the process how the customer perceives the company (a product or service is purchased, delivered, used, maintained or disposed or supplements are bought). Cutting across the stages of the buyer's experience in a matrix, there are the so called levers of utility: the ways in which companies can unlock utility for their customers. Most of the levers are obvious. Simplicity of use, image, and environmental friendliness require little explanation, as well as that a product could reduce a customer's financial, legal or physical risks. A commonly used lever is customer productivity. An innovation can increase customers' productivity by helping them do their thing faster or better.[15] The Buyer Utility Map is an essential element to link the positioning of the offering to the customer to the strategy.[16] It is, however, important to note that it does not evaluate if the current competing elements are superior or inferior to those of the competition.

	Porsche 911	Ferrari F430	Tesla Roadster
0-100	4,8 sec	3,9 sec	3,7 sec
Vmax	289 km/h	315 km/h	201 km/h
Horse powers	350	490	292

Figure 10: Example customer value of sportscars [17]

---

[14] See Kim, W.C. et al. (2000), p. 3.
[15] See Kim, W.C. et al. (2000), p. 3-5.
[16] See Kim, W.C. et al. (2005), p. 118.
[17] See Wikipedia.org (2014).

	Purchase	Delivery	Use	Supplements	Maintain	Dispose
Productivity						
Simplicity						
Convenience						
Risk						
Image/Fun						
Environment						

Figure 11: Structure of the Buyer Utility Map for sportscars. [18] Should a newcomer in the sports vehicle market compete with the classical attributes of such a car or is it possible to create additional value such as environmental friendliness?

In a second step, the current offering of the main competitors can be analyzed. In a search in different internal and external sources, the different stages and layers can be recorded for the product lines and compare them to your company's offerings. Sources can be service catalogs, internal market research studies and/or patents research.

In a third step, potential customers and users can be approached and asked to participate in a survey. The Buyer Utility Map can be broken down to a number of questions, in order to determine in which parts of the process they expect further developments. This method can be used to analyze the current strategy of competitors by mapping their offerings in the matrix. Also, it is possible to match filed patents in order to derive future moves of competing firms (see fig. 10/11).

---

[18] See Kim, W.C. et al. (2000), p. 5.

Linking Business and Innovation/R&D Strategy

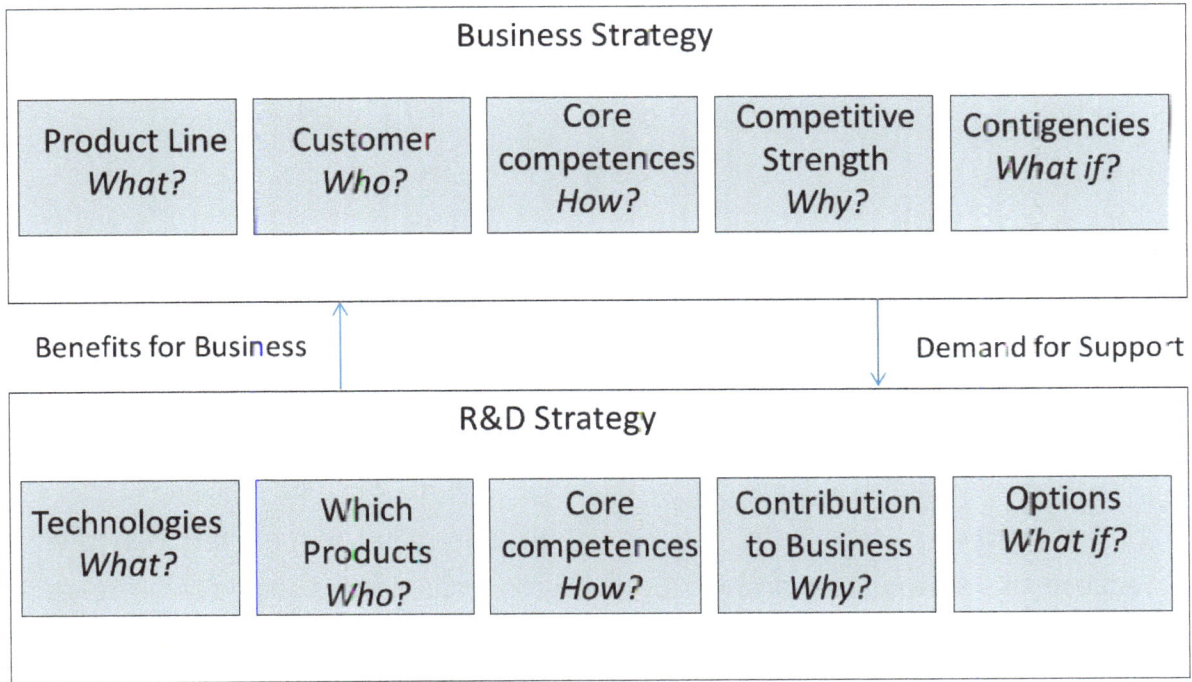

Figure 12: Linking Business and R&D Strategy.

Business and Research and Development must be aligned, although often working with different time horizons. This tool structures the elements of the business strategy and the possible contributions and Support of R&D to it.

A R&D strategy must specify what technologies to master, how the portfolio related to the business and what competitive advantage it adds to the company. It also includes a "how", in terms of timing and risk profiles the products are delivered and how it fits into the available set of resources.[19] It is critical to the success of the company that every strategic activity of R&D is linked to a clear business demand. New products must

---

[19] Loch, C.H.; Tapper, S. (2000): p. 8.

address the right customer segments ; the technology mix must be able to face competitor moves or new regulatory demands. Also, the competences of R&D must match with the future demand of the market addressed in the future (see fig. 12).

Innovation Approaches

Disruptive innovation

Disruptive technological innovations traditionally start out cheap and simple, gradually improving in quality until they challenge incumbents (see figure. 13). Digital platforms such as the smartphone, were enabling innovations that offer customers both a better experience and a much lower price, e.g. free mobile apps' superior to dedicated GPS devices. These "big-bang" disruptions are often unplanned and unintentional. They do not follow conventional strategic paths or normal patterns of market adoption.[20] This kind of innovations is of specific interest in emerging markets as the performance requirements are reduced in favour of a cheaper price. Some companies have special teams or colleges which support the development of disruptive innovations.

---

[20] See Downes et al. (2013): p.4.

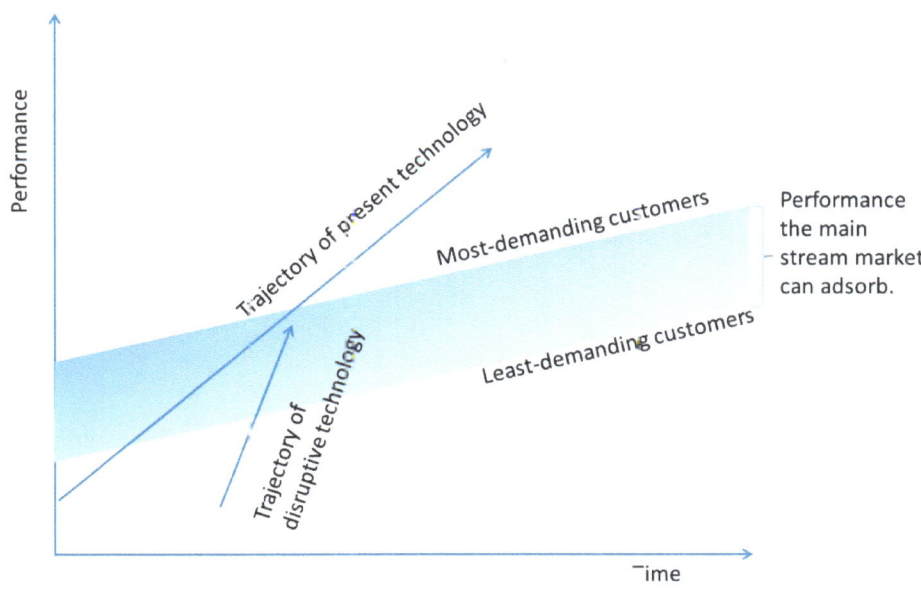

Figure 13: Disruptive innovation (according to Christensen et al. (2000), modified). [21]

Big companies have usually difficulties in developing disruptive technologies as it would potentially cannibalize the current cash-cow. Some use the approach of corporate venturing in order to test such technologies outside the conflictive corporate environment.

Reverse Innovation

Reverse innovation is a concept originally developed for markets in emerging economies and could be highly interesting as strategic approach.[22]

It is based on the fact that products designed for developed countries do not necessary sell in emerging markets with just smaller adaptations. Products must be designed and

---

[21] See Christensen et al. (2000): p 103.
[22] See Immelt et al. (2009): p.3.

managed in the local market and not just modified. Local growth teams need to have P&L responsibility; the power to decide which products to develop for their markets and how to make, sell, and service them; and the right to draw from the company's global resources.[23] The target is to have products which are "local" enough.[24]

Later on these products can be used to access other unserved segments in the developed nations.[25]

Reverse innovation consists of these main activities:

1. Challenge assumptions and follow a clean-slate-approach in designing new products.
2. Move people, decision power and money to the respective market
3. Create a reverse innovation mind-set, by expatriate assignments, immersion experiences and other events.
4. Create separate balanced scorecards for developing countries with an emphasis on growth metrics. [26]

The focus of reverse innovation is typically a search for gaps such as:
1. Performance, as people in developing countries would sacrifice performance of the product due to low income.
2. Infrastructure is developed in rich-world countries but is often under construction in emerging nations
3. Sustainability is a major challenge and presents an opportunity for innovators
4. Regulatory systems in developing nations are sometimes less developed and present lower burdens when registering innovative products
5. Preference is a distinctive driver as e.g. tastes are different in each country.[27]

---

[23] See Immelt et al. (2009): p.4.
[24] See Atsmon et al. (2011): n.p.
[25] See Immelt et al. (2009): p.4.
[26] See Govindarajan et al. (2012): p.48
[27] See Govindarajan et al. (2012): p. 30.

Design thinking

Design thinking is an approach to innovation, where human-centered exploration plays an important role. It involves early prototyping, early user/customer feedback and short iteration cycles.

The steps are the following: [28]

Begin at the beginning: Involve open minded individuals before the direction is set. Create a number of ideas.

Human-centered approach: human behavior needs, and preferences must be in the center of attention. Use human observation when possible. The target is to capture unexpected insights. The formulation of user stories instead of classical requirements helps to formulate context. This enables the developer to understand better the concerns and problems of the end user of the product.

Early and frequent Trials: Use rapid experimentation and prototyping. Use paper-prototypes or simulated software user-interfaces. Use short iterations.

Seek outside help: Expand the team by looking for opportunities to co-create with open minded or critical customers and consumers.

Find talent: use people from interdisciplinary programs or with non-conventional backgrounds.

Design for the cycle: Plan assignments, so that design thinkers go from inspiration to ideation and to implementation in order to experience the full cycle.

Design think leads to frequent iterations and continuous improvement of the prototype and finally product. Indirectly, it forces the team towards agile project management approach. The approach is very common in software development; however, it also offers a variety of possibilities to hardware development as well. Classically, the conception phase takes longer as there is usually a paper-prototype or sketch design However, the prolonged prototyping phase usually pays off, as the resulting development and test will be faster and more targeted. It is not just useful to get

---

[28] See Brown (2008):p. 1-10.

"beautiful" products but also to create user-friendly and efficient workflows and processes.

Open Innovation

Open Innovation is the use of ideas or expertise from sources outside the companies such as universities or other companies.

Before starting any open innovation initiative, it makes sense to evaluate what kind of knowledge your company needs. In some cases, additional ideas or input from consumers are needed; in other companies there might be a need to increase the collaborations with universities. Depending on such an evaluation, a selection should be made (see fig. 14).

	Knowledge	People & Competences	IP	Trials	Key Components	Prototype	Business options
University		X	X				
Institute		X	X	X			
Start-up							
Small and medium enterprises							
Large Company							
Other			X	X			

R&D → Purchase → Development → M&A

Figure 14 : Selection of the required external knowledge. In case of a request for people and competencies from university and research institutes, those could be gained by doing joint research and development (crosses for illustration purpose only).

Common pit falls of open innovation:

Internal resistance: The use of external know-how is often perceived as a clear threat for the internal expert community or R&D. The respective leaders must be involved in the above mentioned decision process e.g. in the evaluation phase to avoid the "not invented here-syndrome"

When cooperating externally, define a transfer strategy. It must be e.g. guaranteed that the knowledge is transferred to an internal responsible. Otherwise there is a risk of depending eternally on external help.

In patent driven industries (e.g. pharma, biotech, etc.), the collaboration might be limited due to IP issues. Confidentiality agreements are mandatory, as well as involvement of the respective legal department.

Structures supporting open innovation are:[29]

- Horizontally integrated companies focus on one step of the value chain. They depend on a network of partners who contribute the remaining steps of value creation. They depend strongly on ideas of their network (e.g. De l) Vertically integrated companies (e.g. most pharmaceutically companies) control all steps of the value chain and typically have strong product development competence. Typically, they practice a closed innovation model, although they might profit from e.g. university co-operations.
- "Informal" structures. Very often open innovation practices can only be implemented by using informal networks as the formal structures of companies frequently oppose to such models. It is however essential that ideas from open innovation must be integrated into the "normal" innovation process. The use of informal structures can only be used for introducing open innovation.
- Decentralized structures allow considerable flexibility. They also tend to develop strong market know-how.

---

[29] Innovation management (2014a), n.p.

- Centralized structured work companywide but lack specific market knowledge. For this reason many companies tend to use hybrid models.

Important steps:

- Align OI with corporate strategy
- Role and actions of top management
- Which skill is required in the organization?
- What is the corporate culture?
- What is the role of IP?
- How to use effectively open innovation platforms?
- How to evaluate the success?

Lean Innovation

Lean innovation intends to increase the output of investments into R&D and innovations by using lean management principles. These principles are long used in other business areas such as logistics or production. Also, it refers to the fact that most product related costs are determined during the research and development phase. It seeks a strong alignment of strategy, customer needs, architecture and design, process efficiency, continuous improvement and controlling of KPIs. Also, often it strives for modular or platform concepts in order to reduce costs.

Nevertheless, classical cost reductions measures in R&D-related environments are often counter-productive, as they create internal resistance and mistrust which heavily harm creativity.

Platform or modular concepts are to be evaluated critically. They be cost efficient but be also a driver of complexity.

Some promising approaches are:

- Improvement of the alignment of business strategy and R&D

- Reduction of administrative burden for researchers to enable more freedom for innovations
- Full-solution- approach instead of product-based approach
- Agile approaches in project management
- Problem reformulation approaches to better understand and solve technical problems e.g. by A3-reports (see respective chapter)
- Triz based approaches produce higher and better output in problem-solving.

Innovation Leadership

Elements of Leadership & Innovation

In the literature, there is a number of recommendations for stimulating innovation in organizations. Barsh et al. (2008) propose the following steps as main elements:

1. Innovation must be on the agenda of senior leaders. It sends an important signal to employees about the value management attaches to innovation. This should also take place on department or team level. Leaders should define the kind of innovation that helps meeting strategic objectives. When senior executives ask for innovations in the gathering of consumer insights, the delivery of services, or the customer experience, for example, they communicate to employees the expected type of innovation.
2. Make better use of existing (and often untapped) talent for innovation, without implementing disruptive change programs, by creating the conditions that allow dynamic innovation networks to emerge and flourish. The talent of employees is often unused and the environment is not favorable.
3. They can take steps to foster an innovation culture based on trust among employees. In such a culture, people understand that their ideas are valued, trust that it is safe to express those ideas, and oversee risk collectively, together with

their managers. Such an environment can be more effective than monetary incentives in sustaining innovation. [30]

4. Set performance metrics and targets for innovation. Leaders should think about two types of metrics: the financial (such as e.g. the percentage of total revenue from new products) and the behavioral. Leaders can also set metrics to change ingrained behavior, such as the "not invented here" syndrome, by requiring a certain percentage of ideas to come from external sources.[31]

5. Making networks more decentralized is another way to improve collaboration and performance. Sharing of information is essential. A larger leadership group with an open and positive mind-set is a distinguishing feature of higher-performing units.[32]

6. Senior executives mention often that making top talent available for projects to meet innovation goals is their biggest challenge in this area. Either they are involved in other business critical activities or they even believe that they do not have enough of the right kinds of talent for the innovation projects they pursue. A different view emerges from below, however. Employees are more likely to believe that their organizations have the right talent but that the corporate culture inhibits them from innovating.[33]

7. The development of leadership skills, such as coaching subordinates and facilitating the collaboration and exchange of information across department silos. Selected managers can be turned into innovation leaders. Identify managers as network brokers and improve their coaching and facilitation skills so that they can improve the capabilities of other people involved in innovation projects. The target is to establish innovation.[34]

---

[30] See Barsh et al. (2008): no pages.
[31] See Barsh et al. (2008): no pages.
[32] See Barsh et al. (2008): no pages.
[33] See Barsh et al. (2008): no pages.
[34] See Barsh et al. (2008): no pages.

8. Create opportunities for managed experimentation and quick success such as test labs. Not surprisingly, this approach is typically the best way to start any change effort in large organizations. Quick success matters even more with innovation: people need to see results and to participate in the change. [35]

9. Explore the opportunities of emerging markets: today, many executives are focusing on outsourcing instead of investigating the specific and demanding needs of lower-income consumers; Western companies can address a far bigger emerging-market opportunity and create the ability to take innovative products and services from the emerging world and use them in new categories at home. Targeting instead the specific and demanding needs of lower-income consumers, Western companies can address a far bigger emerging-market opportunity and create the ability to take innovative products and services from the emerging world and use them in new categories at home.[36]

Furthermore, the CEO of a company is considered as the culture builder. Giving freedom to think creatively and freely can only come from the top leader. [37] A substantial block to innovation is the existence of inhibitors. Inhibitors can be fear of error or retaliation, pressure and deadlines, internal competition or ongoing downsizing. It is a duty of the top management to identify and wipe out such inhibitors if more innovation is a strategic target.[38]

Processes

Technology Scouting

Technology scouting is a systematic approach to gather information in the field of science and technology. Usually, this activity is based on search fields derived from

---

[35] See Barsh et al. (2008): no pages.
[36] See Brown, J. et al. (2005): no pages.
[37] Trias de Bes et. al (2011): p. 228.
[38] Trias de Bes et. al (2011): pp. 233-235.

company strategy (see below). It is critical to evaluate new technologies and review its relevance to the company. Typical sources are scientific publications, fairs, tradeshows, relevant networks, etc. The results from scouting are critical for technology sourcing decisions like licensing, M&A or co-operations. For this reason, it must comprise its potential, risks, maturity of the technology and its fit to the goals of the company. Also, the ability of the company to finalize and market the new technology is critical.

Search fields

Predicting the future is obviously difficult. Nevertheless, it is possible to a certain extend to overview certain "megatrends". Such trends are long term and mostly global developments. Examples of megatrends are the trends to further urbanization, global climate change, the rise of the emerging markets, mobility and so on.

Companies should be aware of these trends and define their future product portfolio accordingly, especially if their development cycles are long. Each relevant megatrend can be addressed by strategic search fields. This means that the company must observe relevant areas of development that have a relationship to its industry and might drive new products or services. These search fields are often an abstract collector for new technologies or desired functions.

Trends of Technology Evolution (TESE)

A very useful and fact-based approach to scouting is the TESE methodology, which is a part of Triz. There are several patterns in the evolution of technologies which can be observed again and again. These patterns are summarized in this approach and can be applied on the product to be analyzed: [39]

---

[39] Park, Hyunseok et al. (2013), n.p.

- Development along S-Curve: After initially fast improving performance, an approximation to a certain limit can be observed.
- Development towards Ideality / more value. E.g. decreasing price and increasing performance.
- Non-uniform Development of System Elements. E.g. Electronics of a car is evolving faster than engine technology (see as example fig. 15).
- Increased Dynamism and Controllability.
- Evolution towards System Completeness
- Evolution of Flow enhancement
- Increasing Degree of Trimming
- Trend of Transition to the Supersystem
- Evolution towards Decreasing Human Involvement

A strategic approach would be to question the current products or services based on these patterns. Where on the S-curve is the product located? Which components develop at different speed? What other functions can be integrated and how could ideality be achieved?

	Pentium 1	Pentium 4	Core i7
Year	1993	2000	2008
Transistors	3,1 Mio	42,0 Mio	774 Mio
Price	870 USD	500 USD	350 USD

Figure 15: Example of Development towards Ideality. Increase of performance while price is dropping. An ideal machine, however, would consume no resources at all.

Stage Gate Process

The process consists in idea screening, concept development and testing, marketing strategy development, business analysis, product development, market testing and commercialization. It is in place in most companies and is considered common practice. Very often, there is a e metric behind the different stages where through put quantities and times are measured as key performance indicators (KPIs) such as ideas per gate, time-market, etc.

The basic idea of the stage gate process is to filter out those ideas early that do not fit to the company strategy, lack of feasibility, possible low customer acceptance or high risk of realization, just to mention some possible criteria.

Common pit falls:

Too many gates / too many decision makers lead to a rigid filter where radical have no chance of realization. In real life, the stage gate leads to a high number of incremental innovations.

Lack of communication of company strategy, goals and search fields: This leads to a number of ideas which are not useful for the company. Also, the high number of non-useful ideas leads to high costs by efforts for review by experts. Finally, they frustrate contributors as they are finally unsuccessful.

Due to the high rate of failure, idea contributors might become frustrated. A valuing feedback is highly recommended to make sure they will contribute ideas in the future.

Recommendations:[40]

- Right ideas in the pipeline: Before adding ideas to the pipeline, ensure that ideas are aligned to the corporate strategy, available skill or capacity, risk profile and potential value. Managers should be allowed to veto on those who don´t fit into

---

[40] Brown, J. (2013), n.p.

the catalog of criteria. This list of criteria should be public. Also a form of self-evaluation by the idea provider is recommended.

- Balance plan and resources: without transparency on available capacity and skill, it is not possible to source both operational and innovation projects.
- Prioritize projects in order to resolve resource conflicts.
- Align innovation projects with business early and communicate launch dates visibly.
- Standardize metrics and execution of processes to monitor efficiency and improve if necessary. Create a community of practice.

Fuzzy Front End

The Fuzzy Front End is the "getting started" period of the new product development processes. It is where the company formulates a concept of the new product and decides whether to invest or not in the further development of an idea.[41]

It may be supported by Front Loading which is a method to develop qualified solutions in industrial research and development. It makes use of simulations and mock-ups without any real prototypes. All possible variations, steps or deviations of the solution are simulated in order to develop a feasible product at a minimum of costs. [42]

It consists in the following steps:

1. Opportunity Identification: business and technological chances are identified.

2. Opportunity Analysis: translate the identified opportunities into implications for the business.

3. Idea Genesis: develop ideas to address the opportunities identified.

4. Idea Selection: management decision, based on fit to the company strategy, business opportunity and feasibility.

---

[41] See Koen et al. (2007), n.p.
[42] See Bytics.

5. Idea and Technology Development. A business case is formulated, based on market estimated, customer requirements, competitors and feasibility of project.

It may consume considerable time, although usually not many resources as it does not involve major investments.

Recommendation:

- Try to fail early. Evaluate many ideas and sort out the best ones and focus on them.
- Involve potential customers or people with real customer insight early and keep them involved during conception phase.
- Have people involved who have a genuine interest in the idea and support them during the process. Business and inventor must be well connected.

Outcome-Driven Innovation

Output driven Innovation attempts to identify important but poorly served jobs and outcomes. ODI focuses on customer-desired outcome.

Instead of assuming what customers want or need, typically product developers determine the voice of the customer (VOC). ODI takes VOC a step further by focusing on jobs-to-be-done rather than product improvements. The objective is to translate customers' real needs into products they really need. states that all companies should find out is what the customers' ultimate output goal is: what they want the product or service to do for them, not how it should do it. [43]

---

[43] See Ulwick, A 2005.

A-F Model

The A-to-F model is not an innovation process, but a list of the key roles that exist in the companies that have shown the best innovation practices in recent years. If a company wants to innovate, it must define and assign these roles to specific individuals and then, having established goals, resources and deadline, let them interact freely to create their own process.

The roles identified are[44]:

(A) ACTIVATORS: These are the people who will initiate the innovation process, without worrying about stages or phases. Essentially, their mission is to initiate the process.

(B) BROWSERS: These are the experts in searching for information. Their task is not to produce anything new, but to supply the group with information. Their mission is to investigate throughout the process and to find the information relevant both to the start of the process and to the application of new ideas.

(C) CREATORS: The people who produce ideas for the rest of the group. Their function is to ideate new concepts and possibilities, and search for new solutions at any point in the process.

(D) DEVELOPERS: People specialized in turning ideas into products and services; they are the ones who "tangibilize" ideas, who give form to concepts and develop a rough marketing plan. Creators come up with ideas; developers invent things. Their function is to take ideas and turn them into solutions.

(E) EXECUTORS: The people who take care of everything to do with implementation and execution. Their function is to implement, that is, bring the innovation under development to the organization and to the market.

(F) FACILITATORS: Those who approve the new spending items and investment needed as the innovation process moves forward. They also manage the process to prevent it getting stuck. Their mission is the instrumentation of the innovation process.

The innovation process will take shape based on the interaction among all these roles.

---

[44] See Trias Bes et al. 2011: n.p.

Resource Management

The ability to take one idea from concept to market is what differentiates innovators from laggards. In order to achieve this, solid processes are required in order to deliver the innovations to market.

Innovators face challenges in:

- Continuously improving consistent processes
- Commitment and management support
- The right software tools

The successful organizations excel in[45]

- Transparency on the use of resources: who is working on what ; identification of potential bottlenecks ; prioritizing of projects
- Combined top-down and bottom-up approaches of capacity planning
- Dedicated responsible(s) for capacity planning and development of skills
- Use of best practices
- Reliable resource estimation and project support processes
- Use of product portfolio management software tools

Evaluation of Innovations

Innovation projects cost money and not any project can be realized. For this reason, it is necessary to choose the "best" projects. However, there are many definitions what the best projects are. In many companies, there are executive committees who decide on the allocation of budget and resources on the projects. In many cases, these allocations depend on the individual opinion of the members and do not follow a certain set of criteria or do not follow a methodology.

---

[45] Kolditz, K. (2013), n.p.

Risk Management

The most important steps are: [46]

1. Recognize that a model needed for making decisions about risk and return. All decisions about how to use an innovation are informed by models, whether formal or intuitive.

2. Acknowledge the model's limitations. Some models turn out to be fundamentally flawed and should be abandoned, while others are still incomplete but can be improved.

3. Expect the unexpected. Even with the best effort and ingenuity, some factors that could go into a model can be overlooked. No human being can possibly foresee all the consequences of an innovation, no matter how obvious they may seem in hindsight.

4. Understand use and user. Some models are suited only to certain applications; some require sophisticated users to produce good results. The model should be well adapted to the context and to the user.

5. Check the infrastructure. The benefits and risks of an innovation are determined not just by the choices people make about how to use it but by the infrastructure into which it is introduced. Innovations and their infrastructures evolve continually, and it is the regulator's challenge to manage that process. The bottom line is that any innovation involves a leap into the unknowable.

R-W-W ("real," "win," "worth it") screen helps to evaluate projects' feasibility.[47]

Is It Real?

A market exists for the product if:

• There's a need or desire for the product.

• Customers can buy it (for example, they have the money).

---

[46] Robert C. Merton (2013): p. 5.
[47] George S. Day(2007): n.p.

• There are enough potential buyers.

• Consumers will buy (for instance, they're willing to switch to your offering).

The product is real if:

• It has precisely described characteristics.

• It can be produced with available technology
and materials.

• It will satisfy the market in its final form.

Can We Win?

The product will be competitive if:

It offers clear advantages over alternatives, such
as greater safety or social acceptability.

• Those advantages can be sustained (for example, through patents).

• It can survive competitors' responses (such as a price war).

Your company will be competitive if:

• It has superior resources (such as engineering or logistics).

• Managers have experience in the market and skills appropriate for the project's scale
and complexity.

• Projects have champions who can energize development teams, sell the vision to senior

management, and overcome adversity.

• It has mastery of market research tools and shares customers' insights with development team members.

Is It Worth Doing?

The product will be profitable at an acceptable risk if:

• Its forecasted returns are greater than costs—considering matters such as the timing and amount of capital outlays, marketing expenses, breakeven time, and the cost of product extensions needed to keep ahead of competitors.

The product makes strategic sense if:
• It fits with your company's growth strategy; for example, by enhancing customer relationships or creating opportunities for follow-on business.

Real Options for Evaluation of Projects

In many companies, the value of new products is calculated based on the net present value. This model is very static and typically assumes a fixed, multi-year investment model. It does not consider value of flexibility and uncertainty. The contrasting Real Options model, although very complex, has the following characteristics[48] [49] [50]:

- Identifies the issues crucial to maximizing value
- Considers the uncertainty of expected cash flows
- Considers the option to extend the duration
- Considers the impact of changes in the risk-free interest rate
- Increases present value of expected cash-flows
- Considers value lost by waiting to exercise

Is closes the gap of fear from uncertainty vs. to seek gains from uncertainty.

Example: A company owns a technology and has the right to exercise it during the next 5 years. The expected cashflow results in a present value of 500 million. The development costs are 600 million $.

→ 500 million - 600 million = - 100 million$

---

[48] Damodaran online (2015)
[49] Leslie, K. (1997)
[50] Aswath Damodaran (1999)

→ This usually leads to rejection of project

Real option: consider uncertainty:

→ 30 percent standard deviation (σ) on cashflows

→ Consider fix costs

→ ROV = $(500 \cdot e^{0.03 \cdot 5}) \cdot \{(0.58)\} - (600 \cdot e^{0.05 \cdot 5}) \cdot \{(0.32)\}$

→ = \$251 million - \$151 million = +\$100 million.

Selection of Innovation Ideas

Regardless of process, decisions must be taken which idea to follow and which ones to end. This is a very critical step as resources should be focused only on the best ideas. The ideas choses should be attractive (= addressing a promising market) and compatible to the abilities of the corporation (=skills, knowledge, culture and ambition to manage the idea).

The graph below shows that the most valuable projects are both attractive and compatible. Area A, which contains the best ideas, only covers a little more than 11% of the total area. Ideas, which might look pretty good in matrix based evaluation methods, will turn out as mediocre (see fig. 16). [51]

---

[51] Fricke (2015)

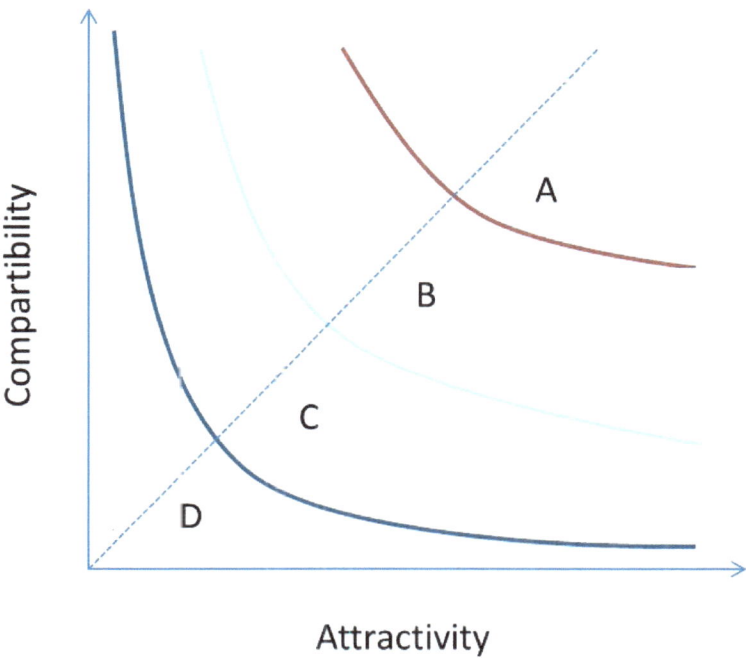

Figure 16 : Selecting the best innovation projects.

Methodology

Quality function deployment (QFD).

QFD is a method for assessing and connecting of customer requirements. It helps to assess if customer requirements are adequately addressed by technical characteristics of a planned product, as each requirement can be linked to technical parameters. This is usually done by the "house of quality"- matrix. Requirements are linked to the planned product parameters, these parameters can also be connected between each other to display positive or negative relationships (e.g. rising costs vs. better product performance).

Additional rows may analyze the weighting of parameters by customers, performance of competitors, complaints, service requests, etc. The density of information is very high (see fig. 17).

Recommendations:

- QFD is very useful for companies with a very structured engineering based mindset.
- It gets very complex and difficult to handle if there are many requirements to be considered. Therefore, it is mainly useful to gather an overview; more detailed specifications must be handled elsewhere. It does not replace specification documents but helps to connect these.

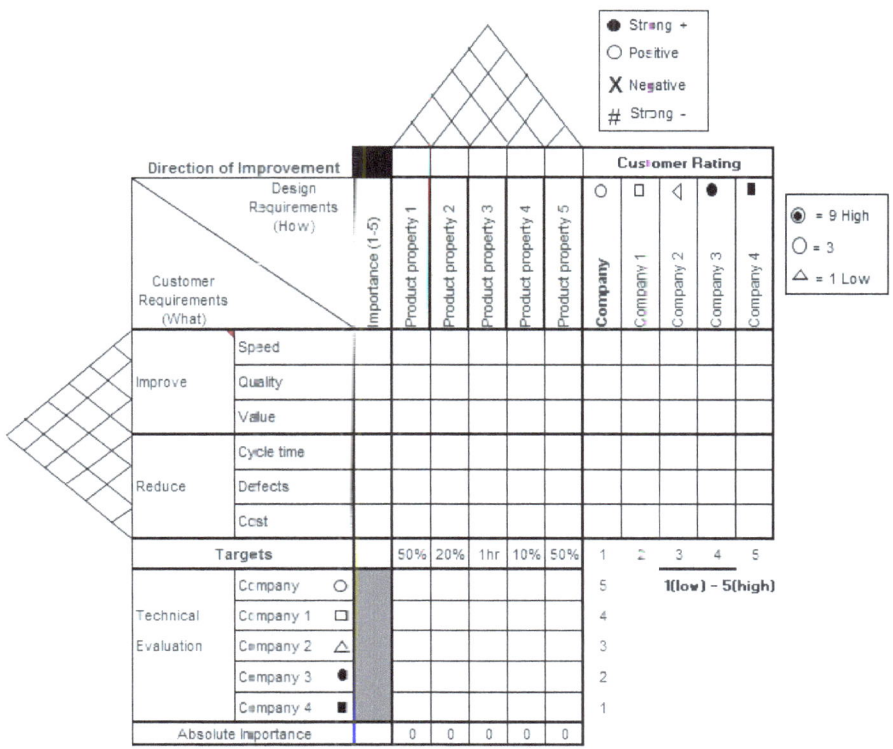

Figure 17: Example of a House of Quality. (Source: Wikipedia)

A3 Report

Humans are used to think in solutions rather than in problems, but, very often we are addressing the wrong problem.

The A3 report is a kind of universal weapon for problem definition. It prevents quick-and-dirty solutions and forces people to a stringent methodical procedure. It is usually printed on A3 sized paper and got its origin in the lean and continuous improvement context.

When discussing a problem, people are first asked to define the problem. When the problem statement is complete, the symptoms are listed. Typically, many of the items discussed during the problem statement discussion will be part of the list of symptoms.

Next, it is very important to become clear which target shall be reached by possible solutions.

A very important part is the search for root causes for the problem. They can later be addressed by the solution proposals and concrete measures. The listing of team members and deadlines will complete the report. Some companies use the A3 report also to manage customer requirements, report project status and other purposes. It is also a very useful tool for moderation and workshop activities (see fig. 18).

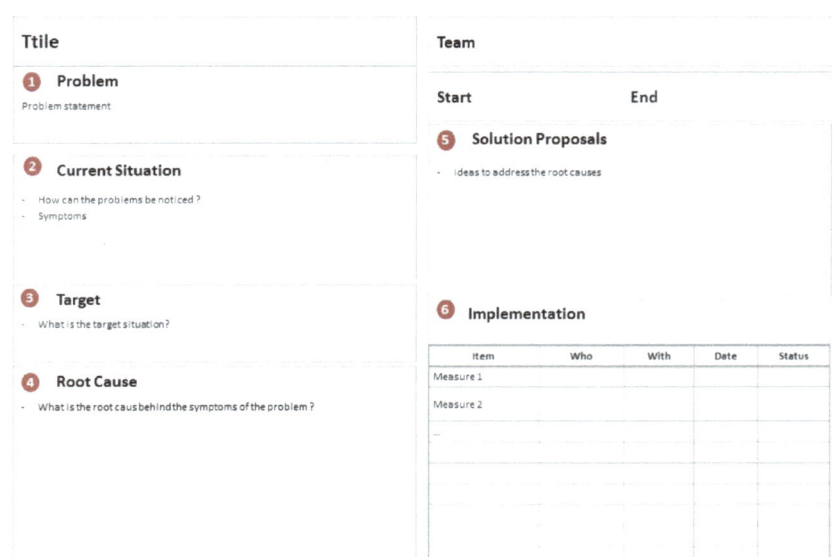

Figure 18: Example of an A3 report.

The Technology Acceptance Model (TAM)

Davis (1985) proposed the Technology Acceptance Model. He proposed that system use (and acceptance) is a result that can be explained by the users' motivation, which is influenced by an external stimulus which consists of the systems features and capabilities. The evolution of the original idea leads to a model where the intention of the individual was introduced, which was influenced by the perceived usefulness and the ease of use (see Figure 19). [52]

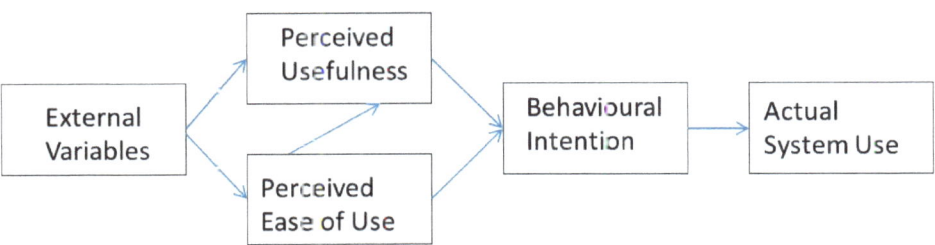

Mobile Payment	Item	Result
Perceived Usefulness	Transaction speed ; Possibility of wider acceptance	0,89
Perceived Ease of Use	Reduced effort ; Convenience	0,91

Figure 19: Function princ ple of the Technology Acceptance Model[53] and TAM analysis for contactless payment versus debit card leads to the assumption that such payment methods may succeed if cost attractive and convenient to use:[54]

A number of evaluations of new technologies were done based on this evaluation model, including e-mailing systems, voicemail, e-commerce, database programs, decision support systems, etc. [55]

[52] Chuttur, M.Y. (2009): p. 2, 10.
[53] Chuttur, M.Y. (2009): p. 10.
[54] See Polasik, M. et al (2012): p.33.
[55] Chuttur, M.Y. (2009): p. 13.

Patent Circumvention

Company seeks to protect their most relevant inventions by patents. Nevertheless, patent documents also provide useful information which would enable to avoid wastage of resources. Circumvention is walking around a competitive patent while not infringing the original. Key is the analysis of the claims of relevant IP. The way of functioning can be best analyzed in a graphical way using the function analysis method (see Chapter on Triz).

Here, the relevant mechanisms are displayed as diagram of components and their functions (see figure 20). Based on this analysis, a design-around process can be started.[56]

---

[56] Li et al. (2013): p. 830.

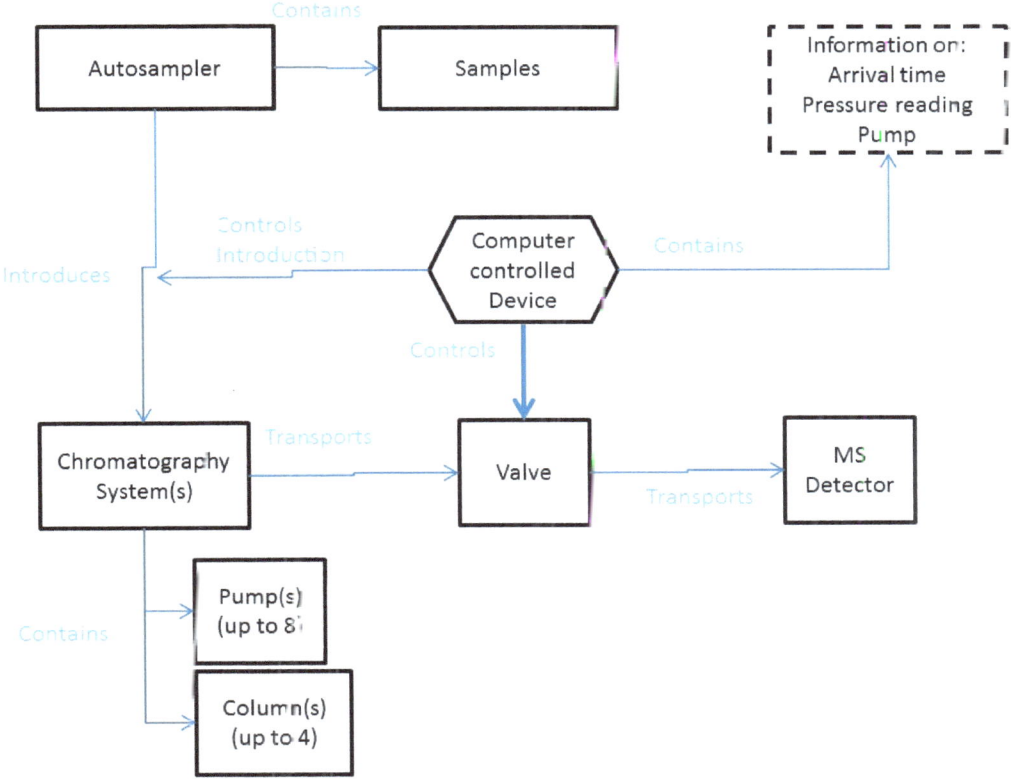

Figure 20: Function analysis of patent application US6635173(B2).

Project Management

The most critical person to realize an innovation after the decision process is the project manager. The project manager will be responsible for delivering the innovation in the desired frame of time, quality and budget. Innovation projects face special challenges, which make it hard to comply with the 3 mentioned targets: the degree of uncertainty is higher, as innovation projects are more likely to face technical problems. It is difficult to recruit the right people with the right skills on the project and keep them there. Budgets are tight and often underestimated. This cannot be a recompilation of all project management methods, but several success factors are:

The project management system and process: big companies usually have a standardized process for project management with regular steering committee meetings for all relevant projects and formalized stage gates which needs to be passed before additional budget is granted.

The project manager itself: is the most critical resource to move the project and solve all related challenges. An ideal project manager should be enthusiastic about the innovation challenge ahead but should be frustration resistant when difficulties appear.

Some critical tools are (list not conclusive)

- Develop a vision on what should be the outcome and communicate it to team, customer and relevant stake holders. An inspiring picture of the aspired project outcome is a very strong motivator.
- Develop a strategy how to get there. Define critical steps.
- Often innovation projects are technology driven. Get a possible customer or internal representative into the information loop as early as possible.
- Agree on rules with your project team. Those can be e.g. the agreement on certain meeting times, the ok of every team member to speak openly without "loosing face", or others. Especially if the team involves people from other
- cultures or the persons don not know each other, it makes a lot of sense.
- Regular (if not daily) team reviews of the ongoing tasks. Decide on the most important ones immediately. Track the status and the degree of completion frequently.
- Limit formal project plans and documentations to an appropriate limit.
- Discuss critical questions with all relevant experts. Don`t take the fasted decision, take the best decision!
- Prototype as fast as possible. If possible use paper prototypes or other cheap models to illustrate and simulate what you plan to do before you start coding or building. This saves a lot of money and developing resources. If applicable, consider training in agile development techniques or design thinking. Alternative, consider recruiting individuals with experience in those skills.

- Show the prototypes to your customer and get him involved. Use the feedback to improve the product and show it to him again.
- Provide a maximum of support so that your resources can focus on what they are supposed to do. Don't hesitate to do the "dirty" work to relieve critical experts from secondary tasks.

Agile Methods/Scrum

In the recent years so called agile development methods were used for technology projects. Among them Scrum is probable the most famous one. Although, this cannot be a full description, a short summary of the process can be done here.

There is a "product owner", who is responsible for the management of the requirements of the product to be developed. He is cooperating strongly with the development team.

The "Scrum-Master" is cooperating with the development team and is monitoring the scrum process. Also, he will solve all kind of obstacles the team is facing. Instead of leading the project, the scrum master is serving the project team members.

The scrum team is responsible for all tasks to resolve during the project. It is usually interdisciplinary. There are no hierarchies and team must organize themselves.

The process starts with a product vision, which motivates all participants. The value for the customer of the product must be clearly communicated. Usually, the vision is developed together with the customer and/or with the management.

As a second step, the release planning is describing the availability of the different versions of the product. The intermediate phases are called "sprints". Between the versions, there are usually incremental improvements; big bang releases are to be avoided.

The product backlog is collecting the product requirements. Initially, it is typically a list of rough requirements, which is detailed in the further advancement of the project. The backlog collects all items, the necessary tasks to complete it, the required effort and the responsible person. Furthermore, it is stating the priority of each item. In the planning for each sprint, the backlog items are collected. Team members take the items of their area of expertise and start working on them. In daily meetings, the advancement on each item is reported and tracked. Problems are discussed and resolved. Every team member is asked to report all activities since the last meeting and what is planned until the next meeting. Additionally, issues which hinder the work are discussed. Those issues are collected separately and are resolved by the scrum master. The advance of the project is described in a burn-down chart.

Advances in the product development are shared with the product owner, who approved the different stages in a review meeting. The product is shown "live".

Another important aspect is the exchange of experience which seeks to improve the development process further by retrospective analysis of issues.

Although there are a number of positive aspects of agile developments, it requires certain attention. The use of a backlog and the "self-service" of team members might lead to situations where team members avoid "unloved" tasks. The number of meetings is very high. Dominant team members might have a strong impact on the result (see fig. 21).

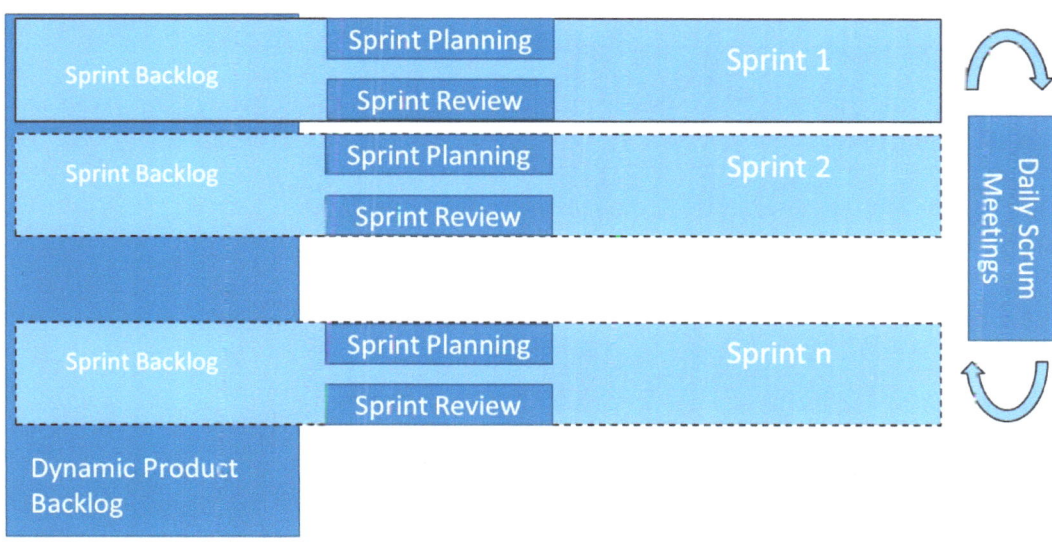

Figure 21: The Scrum process. [57] [58]

Creativity

Link between Environment, Human Factors and Creativity

In order to understand in further detail the human factor in innovation and the underlying need for creativity, I would like to refer in more detail to the componential theory of creativity.[59]

---

[57] Scrum.org (2013) : no pages.
[58] InterFace (2015): no pages.
[59] Amabile, T. (2012): no pages.

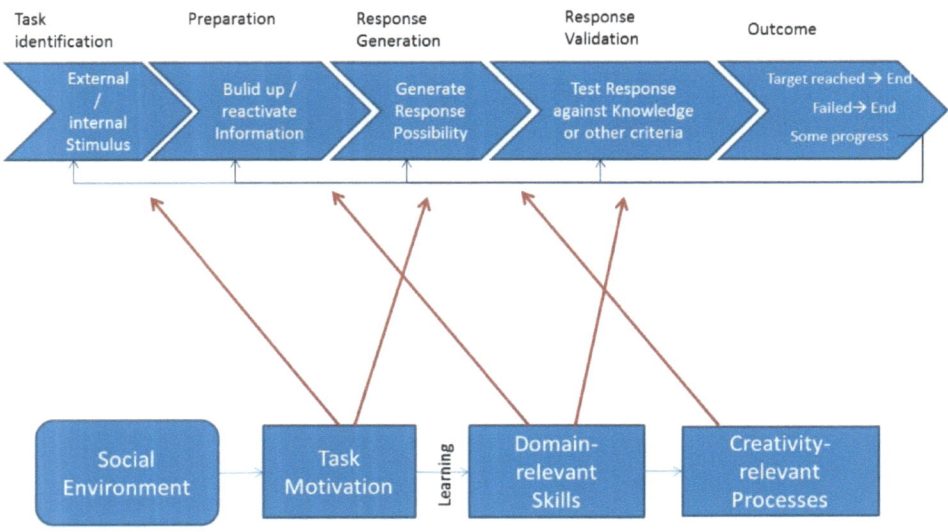

Figure 22: The componential theory of creativity according to Amabile (2012), modified.[60]

The componential theory says that the main elements for creativity can be found within the individual: Task motivation, domain relevant skills, which are acquired by learning, and creativity relevant processes are linked to the human being. However, those elements are heavily influenced by the social environment, which in our case is the working environment. Figure 22show that the different components influence the process of solving a problem. The solving process involves the task identification, search for information in order to prepare a solution proposal, prepare a response and validate it by comparing it with available knowledge or other criteria. The motivation of the individual to undergo such a process is highly dependent on its intrinsic motivation and the respective social environment.[61] More detailed insights on the process can be found in the literature. [62] A good leader tries to provide enough stimuli (task identification) and evaluates the outcome. In case of some but unsatisfying progress he tries to push another loop of the process.

---

[60] Amabile, T. (2012): no pages.
[61] Amabile, T. (1996): p. 9.
[62] See Amabile, T. et al. (2008), no page.

Triz

Triz offers a variety of tool to better understand, analyze and visualize the problem. Futhermore, it references to innovative principles and abstract standard solution approaches in order to trigger out-of-the-box-ideas. Finally, there are fact-based approaches to evaluate future developments.

Triz is the theory of inventive problem solving, invented by the Russian Engineer Genrich Altshuller. He has analyzed thousands of patents and condensed them to a set of 50 methods.

One observation is that Triz provides a way to leave the common solution practices and enables a new kind of ideas by profound analysis and guidance by the inventive principles. Many of the examples for the inventive principles are engineering-focused. It might be useful to pre-select examples relevant to your industry before using it within your context. The method also requires intensive training which might also be a hinder in an industrial context. Nevertheless, the output of high quality ideas is way higher than by conventional brainstorming.

The most know methods are the 76 Standard Solutions and the 40 Inventive Principles. Furthermore, there are further methods tools such as physical contradictions which are resolved by separation principles. The latest evolution is the Ariz algorithm which condenses the inventive process to 85 steps which are applied step by step.

Function Analysis

The function analysis helps to understand better the problem. In a graphical analysis, the different components of a system are listed and their interactions are described. Each interaction is drawn by an arrow (which also differentiates by color if a function is harmful, inefficient, excessive or satisfying. Also, the relationships with parts of the environment are displayed (so called super-system). The analysis is the basis for further improvement of the system e.g. by trimming of components or improvement of harmful or inefficient functions. Also, unsolved functional problems can be used as search terms for a function oriented search (FOS). In such a case, in patent databases the relevant function can be searched and solutions from other industries can be evaluated for use. A specialized application is also patent circumvention (see respective chapter).

The 76 Standard Solutions

There are 76 Standard Solutions available for very technical problems. The problem is formulated as a so called Substance-Field-Model, where the problem is formulated as a model of 2 substances and a field. The 2 substances are also called tool (which tries to do something) and target (the substance to be modified). The field can be magnetic, mechanical, chemical or any other non-material force which is applied to the target or the tool. Within the 76 solutions, there are different groups and you can chose if you want to create or complete a new system, enhance an ineffective one or eliminate harmful effects. Also, there is a group for measuring and detection.

This tool then proposes a number of abstract solutions to the problem model which again serve as effective idea triggers (see fig. 23).

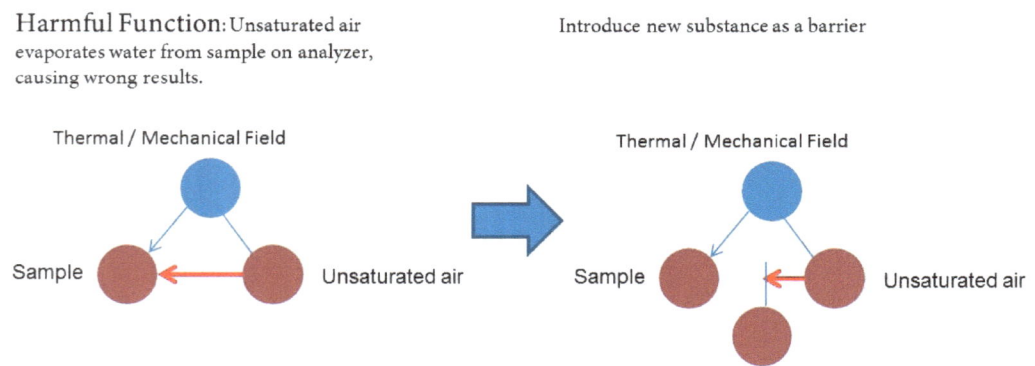

Figure 23: Example Triz (76 Standard Solutions).[63]

---

[63] See opensourcetriz.com, modified.

The 40 Inventive Principles

The most known method are the 40 Inventive Principles. In a first step, technical contradictions need to be formulated. This contradiction matrix makes use of technical contradictions which are then resolved by the 40 **abstract** inventive principles. A technical contradictions a sentence like this :

If I want to increase the performance of a car **then** I can increase the power of the engine, **BUT** the fuel consumption increases.

This typically results in a trade-off (or bad compromise). The power is increased to a certain level until the fuel consumption is intolerable. Triz proposes the use of inventive principles to resolve the contradiction: First, from the concrete problem an abstract contradiction must be formulated. Then, the contradiction table proposes some abstract solution approaches which serve as triggers for a possible solution.

E.g., we have used printed posters with the 40 innovative principles with branch adopted use cases and placed them as idea trigger in a workshop room (see fig. 24).

Principle 10 Prior Action

A. Perform the required change of an object in advance

- – E.g. Sterilize all instruments needed for a surgical procedure beforehand

B. Pre-arrange objects such that they can come into action from the most convenient place and without losing time for their delivery

- – E.g. Pre-deposited blade in a surgery cast facilitates removal

Apply to current Problem

Figure 24: Application of one of the 40 Inventive Principles as trigger to a current problem.

Soft Skills & Communication

Moderating

An essential skill for every innovator is moderation of meetings, workshops or problem solving processes, to mention just a few.

An approach with proven results is the so-called "path2success" method. It uses a simple procedure of questions:[64]

What is the current problem?

Which is the desired future situation?

---

[64] See Eppler, M. J. (2013)

What is the ideal solution?

How would other successful companies like Google, Apple and Toyota etc. approach the problem?

What would be a 3-step approach?

(The last questions are asked in order to stimulate creative and out-of-the-box answers. The results were summarized and not recorded in relation to each question. Also stimulating pictures can be shown for that purpose).

What are likely hurdles?

The process is illustrated in fig. 25.

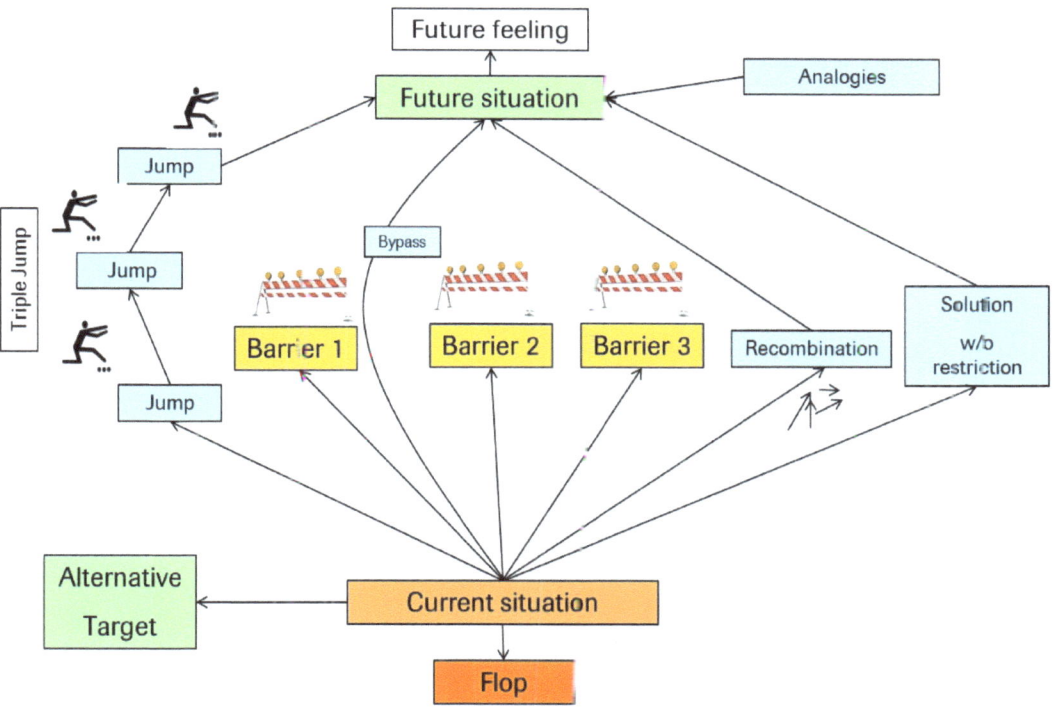

Figure 25: Process of the workshop using the Path2Success Method.

9-Field Thinking

The 9-Field-Thinking or System Operator is a method derived from Triz which is very useful for the moderation of meetings and workshops. It helps to get people into "innovation mode" and re-think the current situation. Typically, the current system to be improved is chosen and placed in the middle of the 9-field matrix. A relevant subsystem and the environment (super-system) are defined. Then, take a look, into the past: how did the system, subsystem and super-system look before (e.g. 10-20 years back)? In a third step try to imagine how the respective components could look like in the future (see example below in fig. 26)!

	20 Years ago:	Today:	In 20 Years:
Supersystem	Modem	Wireless local network	Global satellite network
System	Portable computer, 5-7kg	Laptop computer, 1,5 kg	Wearable computer, 0,5 kg
Subsystem	386 processor	I7 core processor	Quantum processor, cloud based computing power

Figure 26. Example of 9-Field-Thinking: Present, past, future of portable computers.

Customer involvement

New products must satisfy or exceed customer expectations. They must do a job for the user or make him more successful. This is the essence of innovation.

The involvement of customers is dependent on the type of product under development. In some cases it makes sense to involve customers as early as possible (e.g. some software products) in other cases it is limited to usability questions (e.g. in the case of complex products, where the underlying technology has no special relevance for the end user. Geography does not care for the technology of the satellite providing high resolution images. He will only be interested in the quality of the mapping material and consider the satellite as a black box).

A radically new product should provide a new meaning to the customer, giving him a new reason to buy the product. This can be done by using the previously discussed approach of the Buyer Utility Map. Also, design oriented approaches have become popular.

This means:[65]

- Listen: gain knowledge about possible new meanings of the product. Use circles of innovative key users to gain insight.
- Interpreting: Experiment with the knowledge obtained before. Develop proposals, prototypes or mock ups. Share the results and improve again.
- Addressing: leverage key users to explain why the innovation is meaningful.

There are several approaches of documenting customer requirements. Some of the most relevant are:

- Water fall model with user requirement specifications. Requirements are listed in a document. In a functional specification all user requirements are addressed and technological solutions are described. Later, all functions must be tested and

---

[65] Verganti, R. (2013), n.p.

be accepted by the customer or its representative. Relevant for most regulatory industries.

- Quality function deployment (QFD). Table based document which matches empirically weighted requirements with technological characteristics. Comparisons with competitors are possible, as well as evaluations regarding the degree of difficulty of certain technologies.

- User stories. This approach is derived from design thinking and tries to represent the point of view of the customer or end user of the product. It describes in an illustrative way what motivation the user has and what the plans to do with the product.

- A3 report. This tool is structured typically in problem statement, situation, causes, solution proposals and measures. It manages in a very summarized way the problem behind a requirement and avoids by its structure "quick & dirty solutions".

Culture

It's not enough to talk about innovation, or to invest in short term some projects to develop new products or services. Instead, it is critical to make sure that there is a sustainable innovation culture that permanently drives innovation.[66]

It is important to do an honest assessment of the current situation e.g. by doing interviews or performing questionnaires. It is also often enlightening what successful innovators within the organization say, consider their wishes and suggestions.

Transform Culture

The main steps to transform culture are:

- Create a common vision of what your organization will achieve.

---

[66] See innovationmanagement (2015)

- Build a language of innovation, including a consistent definition of innovation and enforce communication about it.
- Develop a strategy (see chapters before)
- Create a connected organization: put people in contact with each other by conferences, internships in other departments, cross-department projects, social networks, etc.
- Sourcing: develop projects with the right persons in the right roles. It is not helpful to generate high numbers of ideas which are not pursued due to lack of the right people to drive them forward.
- Leadership: the right behavior must be rewarded (e.g. by promotions) and the right skillset and potential must be considered in recruiting.
- Don't rely on management by objectives. Setting bonus related targets may increase innovations help as long as innovation is part of the targets, but activities will be skipped as soon as it is replaced.

"Culture eats strategy for breakfast" was said by Peter Drucker. So does it with processes. All kind of structures, organizations or operating procedures favoring innovation are worthless if there is the climate is dominated by mistrust, fear, pressure or poor leadership.

References

Amabile, Theresa (2012): Componential theory of creativity. Working paper, to appear in Encyclopedia of Management Theory (Eric H. Kessler, Ed.), Sage. Editor Harvard Business School. Available online at http://www.hbs.edu/research/pdf/12-096.pdf, last reviewed 23.09.2012.

Atsmon, Yuval; Magni, Max Magni (2010): China's Internet obsession. Edited by McKinsey Quarterly. Available online at https://www.mckinseyquarterly.com/Marketing/Digital_Marketing/Chinas_Internet_obses sion_2546, updated on 03.2010.

Barsh, Joanna; Capozzi, Marla; Mendonca, Lenny Davidson Jonathan (2008): Leadership and innovation. Editor McKinsey Quarterly. Available online at https://www.mckinseyquarterly.com/Leadership_and_innovation_2089, last reviewed 22.09.2012.

Brown, John Seely; Hagel, John (2005): Innovation blowback: Disruptive management practices from Asia. Editor McKinsey Quarterly. Available online at https://www.mckinseyquarterly.com/Strategy/Strategy_in_Practice/Innovation_blowback _Disruptive_management_practices_from_Asia_1558.

Brown, Tim (2008): Design Thinking. Harvard Business Review • june 2008. 1-10.

Cameron, Kim and Robert Quinn (2006): Diagnosing and Changing Organizational Culture. y Jossey-Bass, 242 p.

Cheers Interactive India Pvt. Ltd. (2011): PESTEL Analysis – China. Unpublished.

Christensen, Clayton M., Richard Bohmer, and John Kenagy. "Will disruptive innovations cure health care?." Harvard business review 78.5 (2000): 102-112.

Christensen, Clayton M.; Alton, Richard; Rising Curtis, Waldeck Andrew (2011): The New M&A Playbook. Why you should pay top dollar for a "killer deal"—and other new rules for making acquisitions. In Havard Business Review; Ausgabe März 2011, S. 49–

57.Day, George S. (2007): Is It Real? Can We Win? Is It Worth Doing? harvard business review December 2007

Chuttur, M.Y (2009): Overview of the Technology Acceptance Model: Origins, Developments and Future Directions. In Sprouts: Working Papers on Information Systems 9(37), pp. 1–21. Available online at http://sprouts.aisnet.org/785/1/TAMReview.pdf.

Downes Kouzes, J. M.,Posner, B. Z. (2009): To Lead, Create a Shared Vision. In Harvard Business Review January, pp. 1–2.

Eppler, M. J. (2013): Erfolgspfade. Die Methode der Erfolgspfade für die Ideenentwicklung in Teams. In OrganisationsEntwicklung 1, pp. 82–87.

Govindarajan, V.; Trimble, C. (2012): Reverse innovation. Create far from home, win everywhere. Boston: Harvard Business Press.

Immelt, J. R., Govindarajan, V.,Trimble, C. (2009): How GE Is Disrupting Itself. Edited by Harvard Business Review 87 (10), p56-65. Available online at http://hbr.org/2009/10/how-ge-is-disrupting-itself/ar/1, checked on 18/03/2013.

Jyoti, D. B.,Deshmukh, S. (2006): Balanced scorecard for performance evaluation of R&D organization: a conceptual model. In Journal of Scientific & Industrial Research 65, pp. 879–886.

MacMillan, Ian C. ; Selden, Larry (2008): The Incumbent's Advantage. Harvard business review • October 2008

Merton, Robert C. "Innovation risk." Harvard Business Review 91.4 (2013): 48-56.

Kaplan, R. S.,Norton, D. P. (2000): Having Trouble with Your Strategy? Then Map It. Edited by Harvard Business Review. Available online at http://hbr.org/product/having-trouble-with-your-strategy-then-map-it-hbr-onpoint-enhanced-edition/an/5165-PDF-ENG, checked on 18/03/2013.

Kaplan, R. S.,Norton, D. P. (2005): The Balanced Scorecard Measures That Drive Performance. Edited by Harvard Business Review. Available online at http://hbr.org/2005/07/the-balanced-scorecard-measures-that-drive-performance/ar/1, checked on 18/03/2013.

Kim, W. C.,Mauborgne, R. (2000): Knowing a Winning Business Idea When You See One. Edited by Harvard Business Review.

Kim, W. C.,Mauborgne, R. (2004): Blue Ocean Strategy. Edited by Harvard Business Review. Available online at http://hbr.org/product/blue-ocean-strategy/an/R0410D-PDF-ENG, checked on 18/03/2013.

Koen, Peter, et al. "Providing Clarity and a Common Language to the." Research-Technology Management 44.2 (2001): 46-55.

Leslie, Keith J., and Max P. Michaels. "The real power of real options." The McKinsey Quarterly 3 (1997): 4.

Li, M, Ming, X, Zheng, M, Xu, Z, & He, L 2013, 'A framework of product innovative design process based on TRIZ and Patent Circumvention', Journal Of Engineering Design, 24, 12, pp. 830-848, viewed 30 October 2015.

Loch, C.H.; Tapper, S. (2000): R&D Performance measures that are linked to R&D Strategy. INSEAD Working Papers Series.

Merton, Robert C. (2013): Innovation Risk: How to make smarter decisions. April 2013 Harvard Business Review

Christelle Dujardin; Christoph Schnorr; Matthew Blowfield (2013): Strategic Portfolio Management & New Influencers in R&D Decision-Making. White Paper. Quintiles. 15 p.

Ulwick, Anthony: What Customers Want: Using Outcome-Driven Innovation to Create Breakthrough Products and Services, 2005 ISBN 0-07-140867-3

Osama, Athar (2006) Multi-Attribute Strategy and Performance Architectures in R&D. RAND Corporation, St. Monica, CA. PhD Thesis. 290 p.

Park, Hyunseok, Jason Jihoon Ree, and Kwangsoo Kim. "Identification of promising patents for technology transfers using TRIZ evolution trends."Expert Systems with Applications 40.2 (2013): 736-743.

Porter, M. (2008): The five competitive forces that shape strategy. In Havard Business Review 86, pp. 80–86.

Thompson, Arthur A.; Peteraf, Margaret; Gamble, John; Strickland III, A.J. (2012): Crafting and executing strategy. Concepts and readings. 18th ed. New York: McGraw-Hill/Irwin.

Trias Bes, Fernando de, Kotler, Philip (2011): Winning at innovation. The A-to-F model. Basingstoke [England]: Palgrave Macmillan.

Ulwick, Anthony W. What customers want: using outcome-driven innovation to create breakthrough products and services. Vol. 71408673. New York: McGraw-Hill, 2005.

Zlotin, B., Zusman, A., & Hallfell, F. (2011). TRIZ to invent your future utilizing directed evolution methodology. Procedia Engineering, 9, 126-134.

Internet:

Bytics: http://www.bytics.ch/fileadmin/pdf/Bytics-Infosheet_FrontLoading.pdf

Brown, J. 2013. 7 Tips to Speed Time to Innovation. www. Innovation Management.se.

Braden Kelley (2014) Five keys to making your culture smell better. http://www.innovationmanagement.se/2014/12/17/five-ways-to-make-your-innovation-culture-smell-better/

Damodaran online (2015): The Promise and Peril of Real Options http://pages.stern.nyu.edu/~adamodar/

Reinhard Fricke http://www.innovationmanagement.se/2015/03/19/hyperselect-identifying-top-ideas-and-projects-with-higher-precision/

Kolditz, K. 2013. Improving Time to Innovation. Process is not the Enemy. www.Innovation Management.se

Innovation management (2014a): Organizational processes and structures supporting open innovation. http://www.innovationmanagement.se/2014/04/04/organizational-processes-and-structures-supporting-open-innovation/

Innovation management (2015): http://www.innovationmanagement.se/2014/12/17/five-ways-to-make-your-innovation-culture-smell-better/

Verganti, R. 2013: How to create Products that Your Customers Will Love. Innovation Management.se

opensourcetriz.com (2013:): Idealize harmful functions. http://www.opensourcetriz.com/

Scrum.org (2013): The Scrum Guide http://www.scrumguides.org/

InterFace AG (2015): Scrum. http://www.scrum-poster.de/

Wikipedia (2014): http://de.wikipedia.org/wiki/Porsche_991 ;
http://de.wikipedia.org/wiki/Ferrari_F430 ; http://de.wikipedia.org/wiki/Tesla_Roadster

Bio

Stefan Schaper is Director of IP Management and Innovation at the Penzberg research site of Roche Professional Diagnostics. Since more than 12 years is is involved in the different aspects of Innovation Management in different roles.

After his studies in Biology at the University of Hannover and the National University of Costa Rica he joined Fresenius as project manager and team lead. His main responsibilities were IT implementations, process optimizations and innovation projects. In the following years he managed the innovation process at Bayer Business Services and led projects in the fields of telehealth care and efficiency in R&D support. In his current position Stefan Schaper leads initiatives for the improvement of R&D efficiency, definition of R&D strategy and holds numerous ideation and problem solving workshops. He holds a PhD of the University of Hannover and an MBA.

www.ingramcontent.com/pod-product-compliance
Lightning Source LLC
Chambersburg PA
CBHW050857180526
45159CB00007B/2699

COLOURFUL CLYDEBANK

JACK KIRK

DEDICATED TO THE LATE TERRY PRATCHETT, WHO HAD MORE IMAGINATION THAN ANY OF US

All Royalties from this book will be given to Alzheimer's UK

ISBN-13: 978-1523745708

ISBN-10: 1523745703

Clydebank Library and Egypt

Introduction

Some may argue that the finest building in Scotland's town of Clydebank is the old Town Hall but I would disagree. If it had been finished, perhaps it would have been, but it seems it never was. Below you will see it is a bit lop sided and to the left it cuts off abruptly. Well, it was meant to continue for the rest of the block and be somewhat symmetrical, but it never happened, nor is it likely to. The Town Hall is no longer in use as that, now it is a hall for functions and a museum, the civic functions having headed west to Dumbarton when the town fell completely under the control of West Dunbartonshire.

The Central Library was finished though and is classic in design, built with the financial help of that great philanthropist, Andrew Carnegie in October 1913, it still functions as a library, though these days that means something a bit different to what it used to.

Still, it takes pride of place in this book which started just as an idea when I had a silhouette drawing made for something else. In this case I have filled the library frame with other classical building projects, the Pyramids and the Sphinx.

Iguazu Falls, Paris and Town Hall

You might ask why I added a third picture to the Town Hall and Paris? Easy, it would have left a big space on the top left and I don't like wasting space, but I will at times when I feel like it!

My book, I can do what I like!

Well, within reason I suppose as otherwise I may just get taken away in a little yellow van.

So next is a bunch of castles, starting at the top with Edinburgh, then Dunrobin, dropping down to Balmoral, further to Eilean Donan Castle, and at the bottom left, well, I don't remember as it is so typical of tower houses in Scotland. What have they to do with Clydebank. Well nothing, but my local pub, The Village Tavern in Duntocher on the bottom right, certainly has!

Castles and Crowded Bars

The morning after the Dunti before.

Now don't get the idea that this book is any form of art, the whole thing is a joke of sorts so I, of course, include a few cartoons I worked up over the years. The Pub in the centre is in Duntocher, the drunk elephants somewhere in Africa, and the mountain could be either N. America or maybe the Alps. I don't really remember!

Below is not so funny. Maybe a paint job on the outside of the Radnor Park Hotel might improve it enough to save it for it has been up for sale for over a year, and already has started to get that abandoned look. Like its just waiting to commit suicide by wreckers ball!

The place itself is quite impressive as can be seen by the drawing below the Yosemite version and has probably the best location of any place in the whole town, right at the top of Kilbowie hill. Now that would also make it an ideal spot for perhaps a few high end houses or flats, but maybe the asking price is too much for builders as it could only be a few. The hotel footprint is not all that large so when taking all those factors into account, it possibly and hopefully stands a chance of surviving as a hotel.

Radnor Park Hotel & Yosemite Park

Radnor Park Hotel in 2010

On the next page we have another establishment in the drinks trade which is up in Duntocher, not as I have shown it in front of Angle Peak in the Canadian Rockies. It is certainly alive and well and not in any danger of folding as far as I know, but then again, I didn't know about the Radnor until it was already closed. These days pubs and hotels do not seem to survive too well. Maybe best to get a picture of it on record while I have the chance, for ten years back, before I really started my little manipulations, the Duntocher Hotel shut down, and I have yet to trace a good picture of that place.

Glenhead Tavern with Angle Peak

Not all of my drawings are messed about with and the next needs no manipulation at all. It is a classic looking building even if originally, and it has not changed a lot over the years, it was little but the station building for Riverside Station, opened 1896, closed finally in 1964 and turned into flats years later. The railway itself was built by the Lanarkshire And Dunbartonshire Railway to serve Clydebank and the John Brown's shipyards next door, and now the last part of it, like the yard itself, sits isolated from the most of the town. It had three platforms and a spur ran off under Glasgow Road up what had been a feeder canal to the Forth and Clyde, now the present Argyll Road.

I never knew it existed till I was around that way one day looking for a printers shop and turned down the street the wrong way and I would bet half of Clydebank don't know it still exists and most probably don't even know it ever did exist!

Go see it yourself- if you can find your way in!

Riverside Railway Station

Now another one which is a little personal, the Kilbowie Church with Alicante infill. Never been in the church, even though it's now a restaurant, but I've been in Alicante a number of times over the years. Look carefully and you'll even see me there!

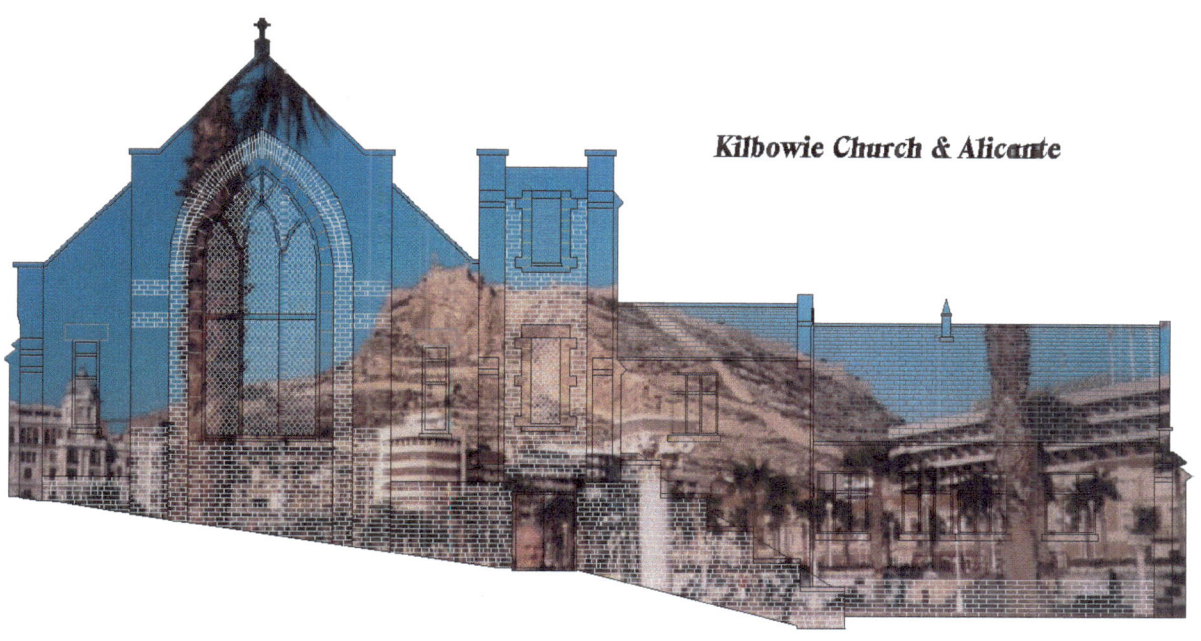

Kilbowie Church & Alicante

At times it may appear that I have wandered in to the realms of madness but though at times that is true there is a connection to the main theme of this book. The "Spaceship" below is not from science fiction, though perhaps the architect who designed it may have been a fan. When I first came across the aerial view of the Clydemuir Primary School in Dalmuir and I thought the aliens had landed!

Maybe they have, there are some strange exotic creatures wandering around the shopping centre these days!

Education of a Strange Kind

You might ask what a tartan clad straddle carrier is doing in a book about Clydebank? Easy. The tartan is the Kirk Tartan. I live in Clydebank. QED!

Kirk Tartan & Straddle Carrier

Roman Road Armadillo

Nothing to do with each other except the shapes sort of fitted. These semis just off Roman Road are already painted white so it is a blank canvas just waiting for an odd shape like the concert hall in Glasgow and a brilliant sunset

I think this was the second photograph I put into an outline, and a bit appropriate as well. St Mary's church inclosing Vatican square! Not that I am all that religious, the opposite in fact, but my dislike of extremist religion is somewhat tempered by the amazing architecture that has been created in the name of religion. I am not crazy keen on some of the more modern sort, though given the choice of a brick built fairly modern church built in a traditional style or one of these weird concrete flat buildings that seem to be in vogue, I'll have the bricks and tradition anytime.

St Peters in St Marys

There is nothing traditional nor religious about the next inserted drawing. The Titan crane once dominated John Browns shipyard in days when Titans strode the banks of the Clyde and built ships like the famous Queens and the tragic HMS Hood.

The Titan was saved though and is now open to the public and you can get a lift up to the top for a superb view of the town and the river. When I was serving my time I helped to build our works crane and have been up a few since then, but strangely not this one on my doorstep. Maybe some summer's day.

It is enclosed by a milling machine which I also used as an apprentice and is much easier to get to than the top of a crane!

The Crane in the Mill

The Ettrick Bar in Old Kilpatrick encloses the Bailytong Elevator and the spectacular surrounds of this gorge, deep in China. I know the Gorge area is probably of more interest than the pub so I have constructed a second picture that shows the pub set in the gorge picture. You need to know more about either, look them up. Yes, that is the Elevator with a two floor building on top at the left hand side so just think about the height!

The Ettrick in China

Going fast past Fitzys

Now motor bikes are not my sport but I have to admit there is an ancestral link. A few of my immediate ancestors ended up dead on them! Best stick to doing pictures of them then. This is the past multiple world Champion, Valentino Rossi, superimposed on the house of a friend, in Auchentoshan Avenue, who idolises him. He'll know who I mean!

Maybe not as impressive is my own block of flats at the end of Mallard Road and it encloses the esplanade of the small Spanish town of Albir Playa near Benidorm where the wife and I spent a lot of time from 2006 to 2012. Those were good years there and Albir is a beautiful place without the noise and babble of its noisy next door neighbour. I'll return to it again as some things in the village are too lovely to ignore.

A Mallard Duck in Paradise

Literary Sunset

A compilation of Clydebank Central Library and Duntocher Library and a sunset from god knows where, but it does have a good effect! The Central library will get more than its fair share of exposure but then, it is such a fine building it deserves it.

Oceanfield flats & Blackwaterfoot on Arran

Just off the Great Western Road these flats house another friend and he should recognise this scene as he spent some time round about there refitting a place. , to my regret, managed to drive right through Blackwaterfoot years ago without really seeing what the place was like, then again, maybe he won't recognise it either as I believe it was under a deep cover of snow when he past!

The Old Hamilton Memorial Church on Glasgow road lies forlorn and abandoned the last time I saw and up for sale for less than a hundred thousand. Contrast that with the houses of Parliament and Big Ben the repairs to which started off at over three million in 1914 , jumped to seven million in 2015 and without doubt will continue to rise. Okay, the palace of Westminster is a lot bigger and a lot older and provides an important function. It keeps a lot of blowhards in a job and provides them with a cheap bar to drink in, all subsidised by the taxpayer!
Still, it makes one wonder what the hell is going on. If I make a fortune out of writing,(fat chance!!!) maybe I'll save it –and build a bar out of it?
Or maybe just fill it up completely with concrete so nobody can knock it down!

Hamilton Memorial Church
& Big Ben

Now Picasso's Women of Algiers fetched £102.6 million in a recent sale, which I found unbelievable but there are crazier people than me out there. I made that comment in the pub and was asked if I could do better? What is better? I mean, it's very subjective valuation.

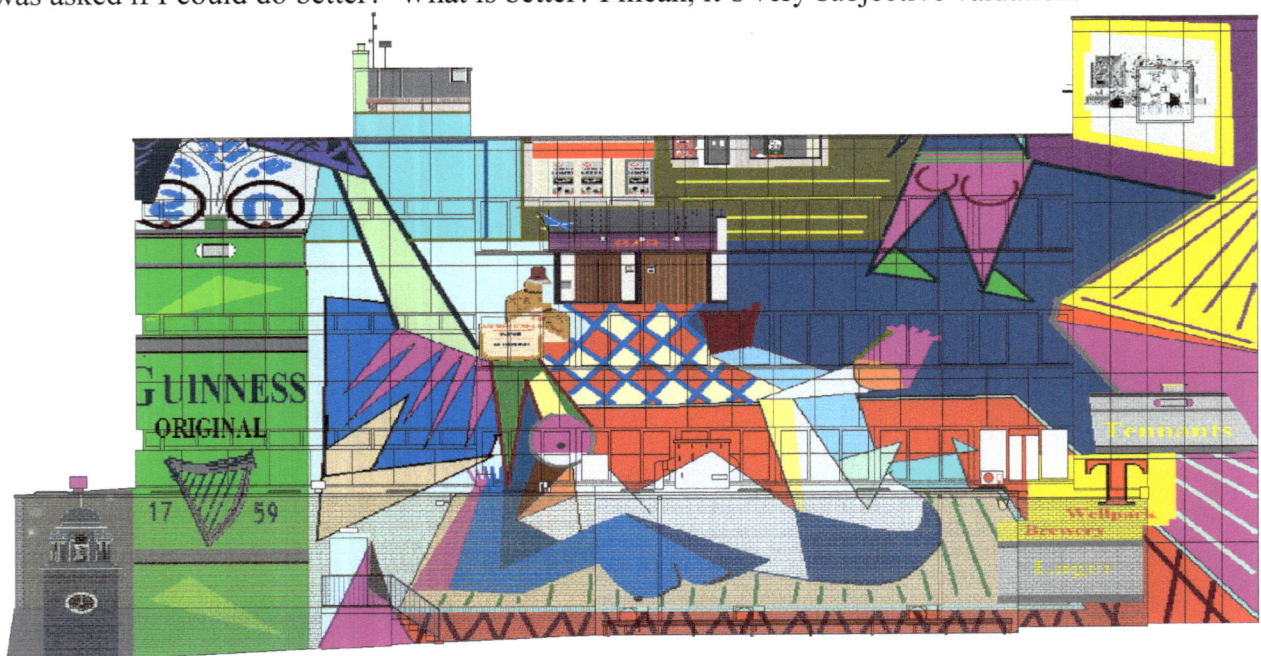

Girls of Clydebank in Jail!

Anyhow I did Girls of Clydebank and showed it in the pub and nobody was impressed, so I've put them in the Clydebank police station for now as I suspect they might feel at home there!

Two Queens

Half the towns in Scotland have a Queen Mary Building but Clydebank has a better claim than any so here's the one in Duntocher with the real queen Mary in front of it!

There are probably a few people would agree that a bulldozer would be the best thing to happen to all the high flats in Clydebank, or most places for that matter, but that is up to them. Or down to them for that matter. But they do make a statement and this group of flats near the top of Kilbowie hill certainly will provide some spectacular views, all the way down the Clyde to Arran I imagine, as do the hills behind Clydebank, where I have had that view. Everything has some purpose!

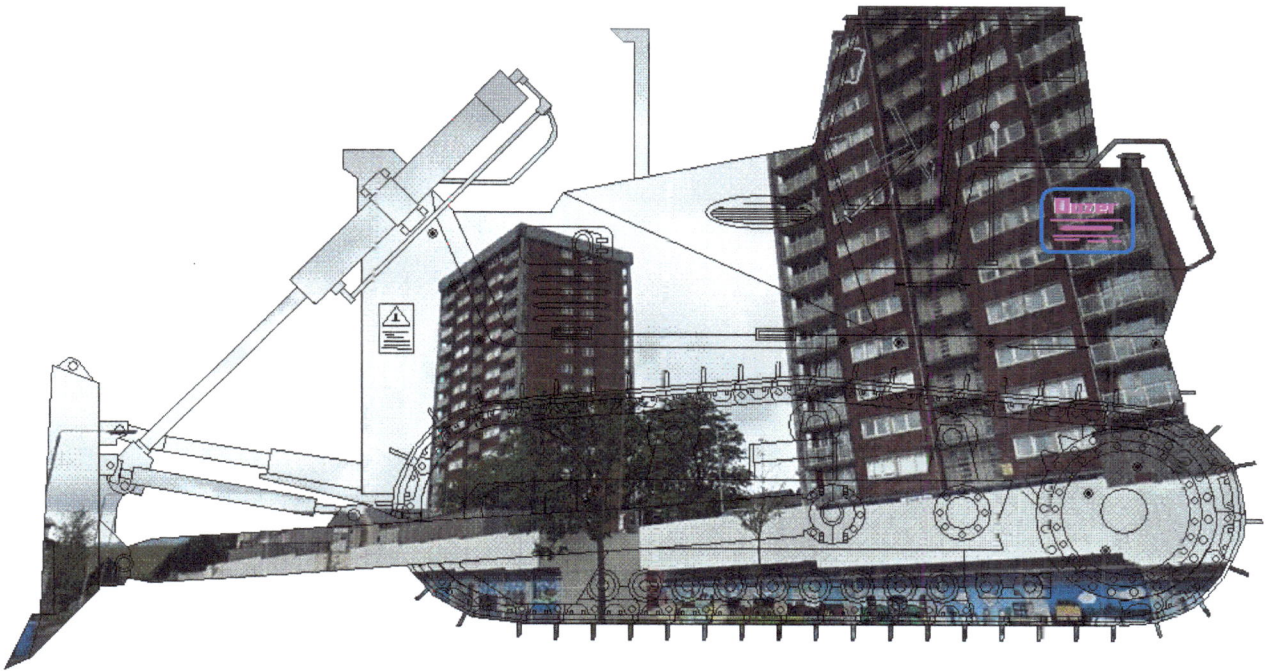

Bulldozer with Church Street Flats

Double View Trinity Church and across behind it.

Just because I used a church to depict a church does not set things in stone. Never do that! I have use d the trinity church on Roman Road simply to frame the scene from not too far away, overlooking Milton Douglas Road and the small white square of the West Highway hotel near the top left. To some that might seem irreligious, to others, maybe just a different religion.

Just to prove that nothing means anything I have used St Mary's again showing a temple in India, just an alternate way of bringing some colour to the place!

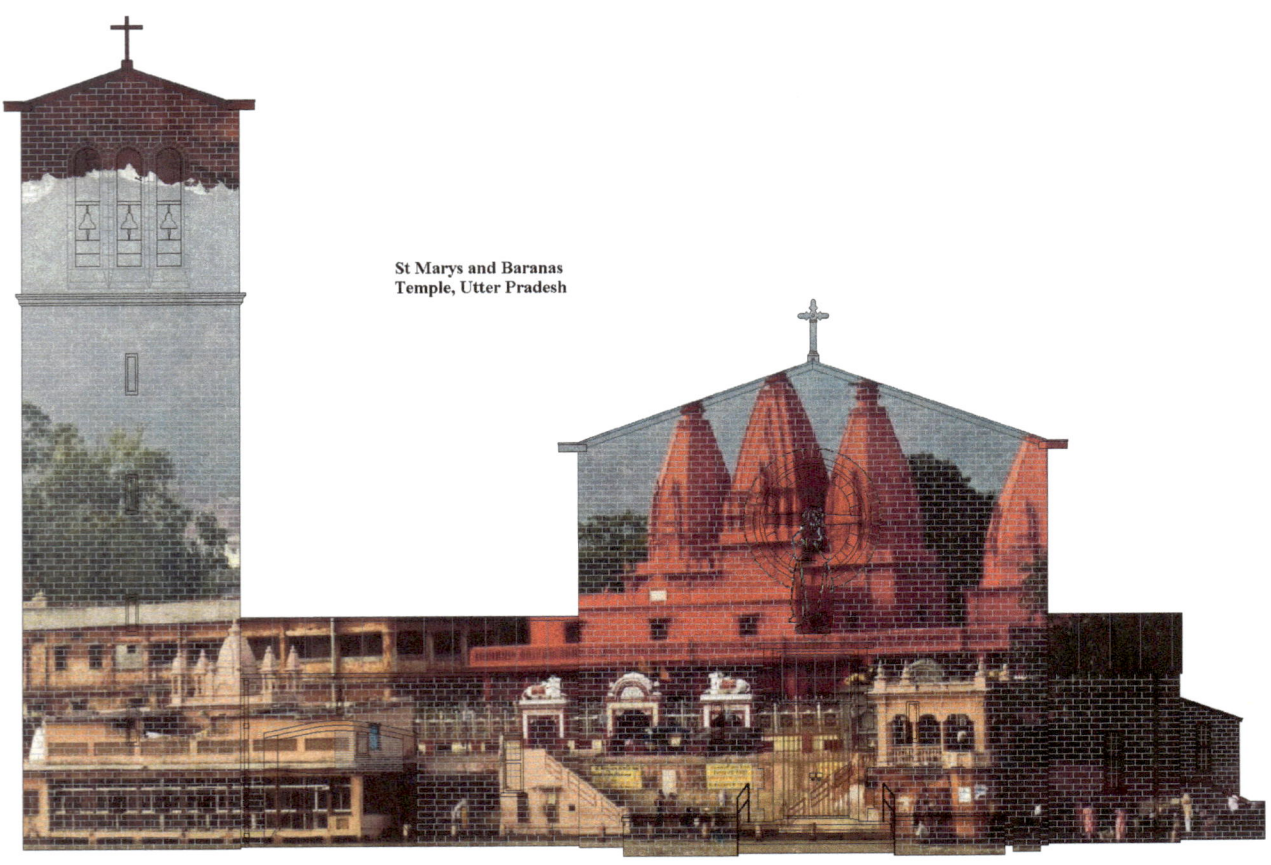

St Marys and Baranas
Temple, Utter Pradesh

You might wonder why I would enclose the Coop Store across from Clydebank Station in a shearing machine, but don't, because I don't really know either! I just thought it was appropriate. Shearing machines of this type were hardly unknown in the area, every shipyard would have a few, most a lot bigger than this, and Singers in its heyday would also have them. I worked on one at times all through my apprenticeship and its probably the nearest I got to shearing a finger off. Just a bit crushed to remind me to be more careful!

Maybe that's it, maybe I caught my finger in a door at the Coop and subconsciously remember it?

Or maybe I didn't.

The Main Coop Warehouse & Shearing machine

Way back around 1987 I visited both Sidney & Melbourne and I have to admit that Melbourne I was not all that keen on. Too quiet for those days, so I have livened up one of the finest houses in Dalmuir with a picture of Sydney Harbour taken from the Opera House. I had not noticed the pigeon sitting on the top of the lamppost at the time but since then realise it was the best piece of luck I could have had!

Melbourne House though is worth a visit as it has a history, it was built for the foreman of Beardmore's shipyard.

Sidney in Melbourne House

Not many ships built on the Clyde these days but I'm glad they built this sculpture of HMS Ramillies down at Dalmuir to honour the Beardmore shipyard that used to be there. I doubt if Tom McKendrick would grudge me the use of his fine piece of engineering art.

The ship in front was my second last, the Grampian Protector, and has no real connection to the area except myself as it was a Rig StBy boat running out of Aberdeen and built in Norway. It was also the last ship I was on before moving to the area and is likely to be melted down into scrap by now, maybe to build another steel sculpture?

Beardmore sculpture and Grampian Protector

Now steel structures are not what you want if there is lightning around-unless you are on a ship! I have seen a lot of electrical storms from ships, and the ships are frequently hit, but seldom damaged as there a perfect earth because they are sitting on water. So the story goes but that is no consolation if you are in the middle of the fireworks!

Lightning in Hillend Crescent

The lightning storm I remember best was on a big bulker back in 1993 when we were travelling north up the Bahamas Passage and my wife and I sat out the back of the accommodation watching a spectacular electrical storm, no rain though, a few miles behind us and getting nearer. There was a short trail of ships behind us so we could watch the progress of the lightning and when one big flash hit the sea between us and a ship half a mile behind us it was definitely time to go inside! I somehow don't think Hillend Crescent in Duntocher has never had a show like that!

Bali Temple & Dalmuir Church

Sometimes the gable end of buildings is more interesting than the front and this was the case with the Barclay Church in Dalmuir, but even then it was fairly plain. Paint a picture of a Hindu temple on a tiny island near Bali on it and you can see they beat our church building by a country mile! Well, the Scots churchgoers were always a dour lot!

Overtoun Court in Dalmuir, or for that matter any of the high flats around the place, will never be pretty but given that, when combined with an MAN B&W 900 mm bore engine, they do have a bit of style. Takes something to do that! Maybe I have just invented a new style of Architecture, Brutalist Dieselist Jackist, with flying buttresses and superchargers!

Could be that would bring the tourists to Dalmuir, but if not, would certainly employ some of the ex-shipyard workers, the few that are still alive!

Dalmuir Big Engine

Now Faifley has not a lot of unique buildings nor many with even very good shapes but I like the two blocks of flats in Abbeylands Road. Given a little paint and some effort we could always use one of Scotland's most iconic structures to brighten it up, and confuse, because I had already used some Edinburgh buildings and a background of a very red sky to make up a collage of colour.

Edinburgh Abbeylands

Next we have the block of flats called Lomond View. I have no doubt the Loch of that name is not visible from the flats but maybe Ben Lomond is, then Ben Lomond is visible from places way out in Lanarkshire! No doubt again that Dunvagen Castle can't be seen from the flats but I imagine that The Village Tavern in Duntocher in the bottom right of the picture is, and it is nowhere near .
Hardly matters, does it?
Well, that is Loch Lomond in the middle at least and the old steamer, the Maid of the Loch which I hope is still fit and able to ply the waters.

I expect there are a few lathes in Clydebank College but I'd bet that nobody before thought of putting Clydebank College inside a lathe! I mean, nobody, but nobody is that crazy. Except maybe me!

I have worked on approximately seventy lathes in my lifetime, one for every ship except three little ones that did not have them, plus two or three in Gib Dockyard and maybe four or five while serving my apprenticeship. That also works out at approximately one for every year of my life so maybe I'll have to find another few to give a spin!

Turning out the College

Said it before and will say it again, the Central Library is the finest building in town so why not give it a better location? Place it at the edge of s nice grassy bank with a spectacular mountain and a sunrise behind it and there we are! I wouldn't object to that as long as it was kept just down the road from where I live, nor would to many people in the town object to a mountain like that just across the river! Think of the tourist trade!

Singer and the Holy City

I produced a small book on the buildings of Duntocher and adjacent areas last year and all the buildings in the Village I had drawn were in it. Except one in Carlieth Avenue.

Sorry about that John, so now you have your gable end framing Singer's clock which you worked under years ago and the "Holy City" behind it. Not the one that was destroyed during WW 2 but Jerusalem itself.

There is a connection between the Trinity Church on Roman Road and the view framed in it. Just climb up the hill and walk round a little and there it is, looking over Milton Douglas Road with the small white square of the West Park Hotel near the top left.

In the Blue picture below Trinity appears again along with another few buildings in Duntocher.

Trinity with Trees

Cold Dawn

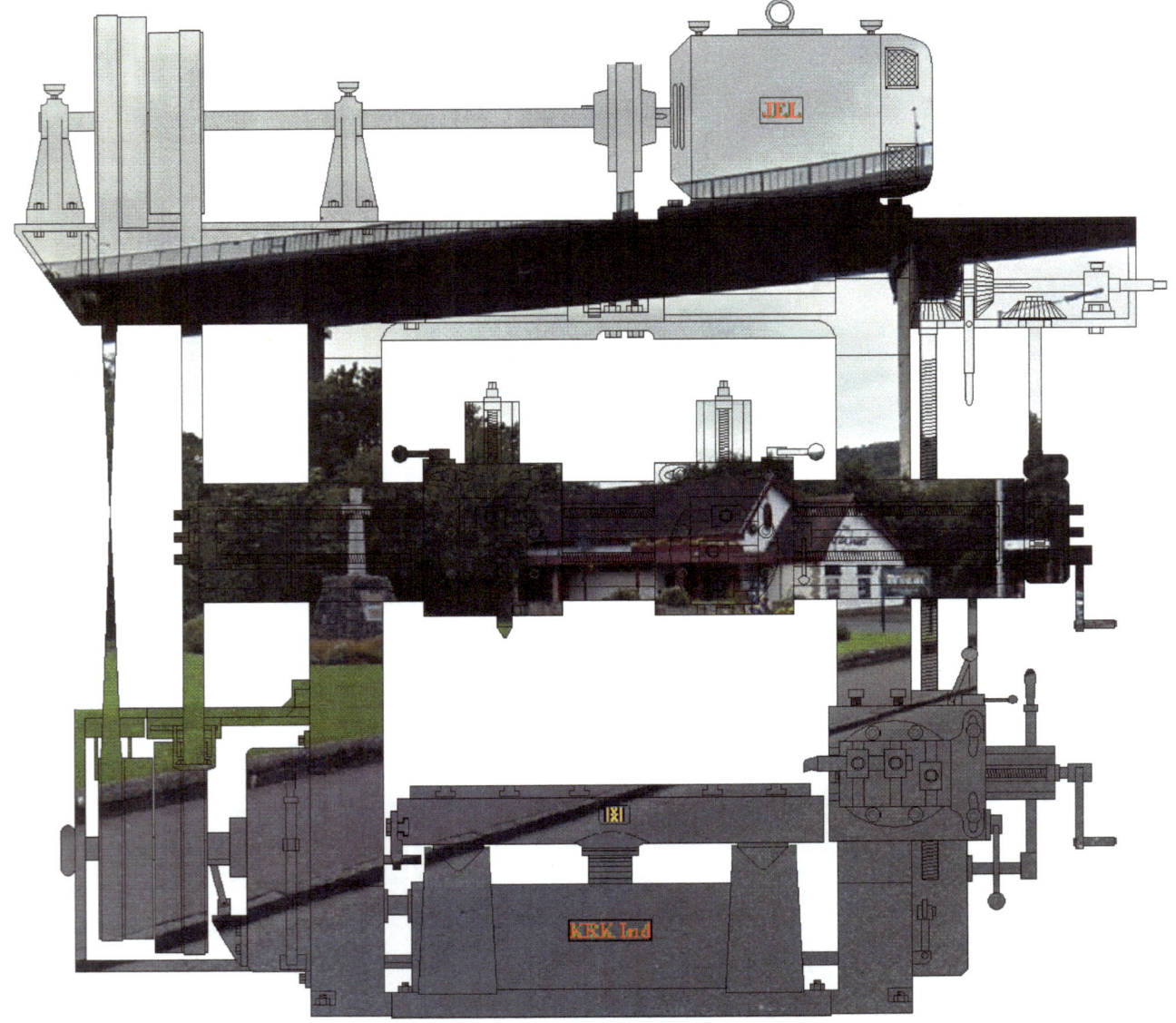

Bridge, Battle, Booze & Bloody-mindedness

If you are wondering where the bloody-mindedness comes in, the planing machine that is used for a frame was my pet hate when serving my apprenticeship. I will not elaborate on that but instead point out the picture is of the Erskine Bridge, the Old Kilpatrick war memorial and the Glenn Lusset pub. No connection at all to a planing machine except my quirkiness!

Then we have the Duntocher Vietnam Mountains with the West Park Hotel hanging over the White Cliffs of Clydebank. Careful with the parking! How much better would it be if you could sit outside and watch the dolphins play when drinking your Pina Colada, rather than have an eighteen wheeler hurtling past belching exhaust fumes all over your pint?

Mind you, I'm not all that fond of Pina Coladas!

People say I should be used to the heat having worked abroad so much. Well, yes I have been in lots of really hot places like Canada, Russia, Finland and Sweden in winter, but I don't think we Scots ever really get used to the heat like the wife and I suffered in Crete one summer. 44 deg C is excessive and the first thing we did was move from a hovel down in the town to the hotel shown here at the breezier top of the town, and then a few days later into an air conditioned room. And it was still too hot during the day to anything.

So I've moved the hotel down to a house in Dumbarton Road in Old Kilpatrick where it has been known to be a bit cooler!

Neo Ikaros in Old Kilpatrick

Town Hall by Midnight was done some years ago for a library competition and didn't sell. I still have the framed image printed on A3 and waiting on the first ten million dollar offer!

It was a sort of accident anyhow when I finished the original drawing and accidentally reversed the colours. A moon and a few stars added and voila, a work of art! Or a work of something.

Now that sounds so simple but really the town hall drawing took a while to do so if you fancy doing the same thing be prepared for a bit of work first. And don't expect the ten million dollar offer!

Town Hall By Moonlight   *Jax*

Clydebank Baptist, Kyoto Buddhist

The old Baptist church in Alexander Street makes a good frame for a Buddhist temple in Kyoto, Japan. I always marvelled at the daring of them for making such ornate temples and castles which look like a good gust of wind would knock them over, but were obviously ancient, and this in major earthquake and typhoon zones. Then I was on the south island of Kyushu and at an old castle there, and found it was built of reinforced concrete and steel. It had been rebuilt after being bombed to next to nothing during WW2.

I suspect rather a lot of these ancient temples have been rebuilt, maybe several times, but I am glad they done it in the old style. Much better than our dull concrete modern buildings.

Just to prove Clydebank is not all concrete and industrial wastelands the next frame contains woodlands up the back of the town. If you are ever up there and bump into a monster like this, don't worry, it is a concept forest harvesting machine built in Finland a few years back. Then again, it has no business up in those woods so maybe you should worry! I know I would probably run like hell!

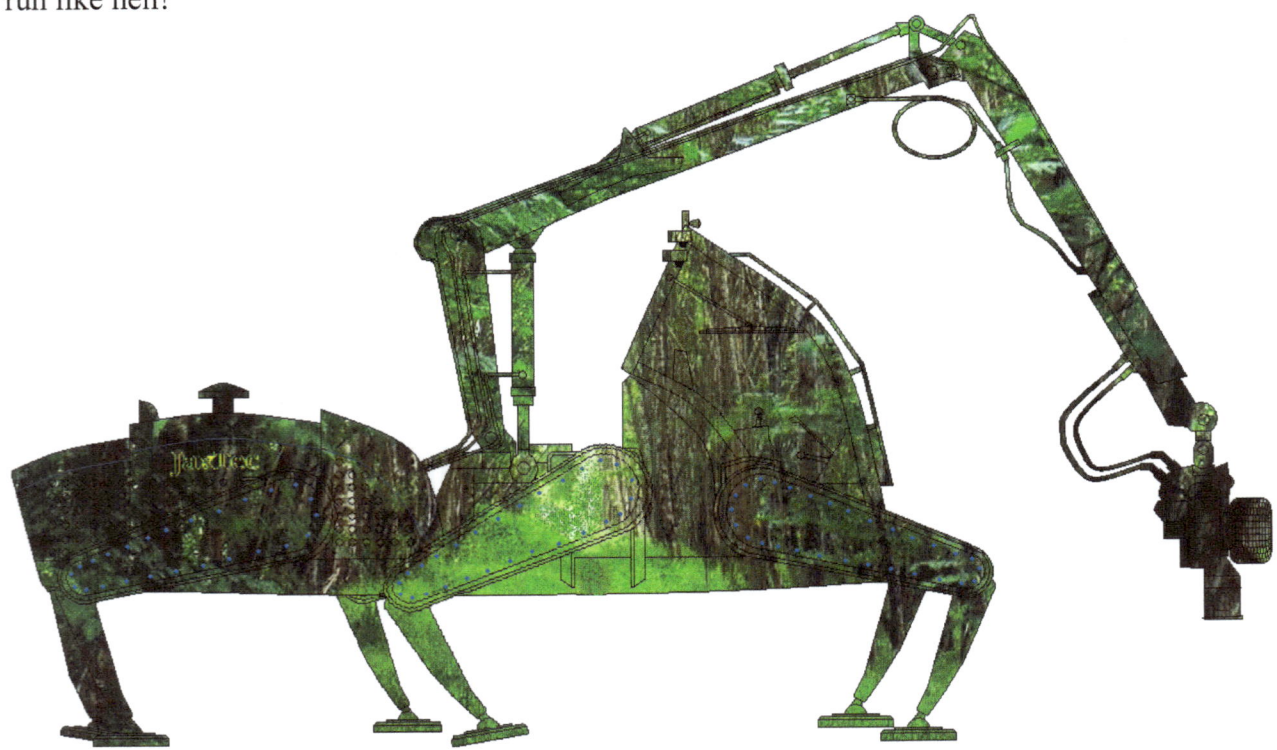

Creatures of the Wood

Dalmuir has its cold days without a doubt but the picture of the Park Road church with a great ice mountain behind, mounds of snow and icy ponds in front, is an illusion. The mountains are desert buttes and the icy ponds and snow are warm ponds and desert scrub! Then reverse the colours and we have the Arctic Effect!

Sometimes this works well and I think this is one of them

William Beardmore was a well known shipbuilder in Dalmuir many years ago but it is less known that his company produced aircraft, mainly Sopwith Pups, during WW1. The present day Jubilee hospital and Hotel is built on the shipyard site so why not do a flypass!

Beardmore Legacy

Way back in 1846 Cornelius David Krieghoff painted the view looking down the Clyde from Dalnottar Hill towards Dumbarton Rock. He was neither the first nor last by a considerable amount, the view is famous. It is also extinct unless you walk over the Erskine Bridge or go over on a double decker bus!

This time I have layered it onto Beardmore House and the building next door, in Dalmuir, and I must admit it seems to give a good old fashioned effect on stone buildings.

Well done David, your painting does you credit.

Dalmuir & Dalnottar

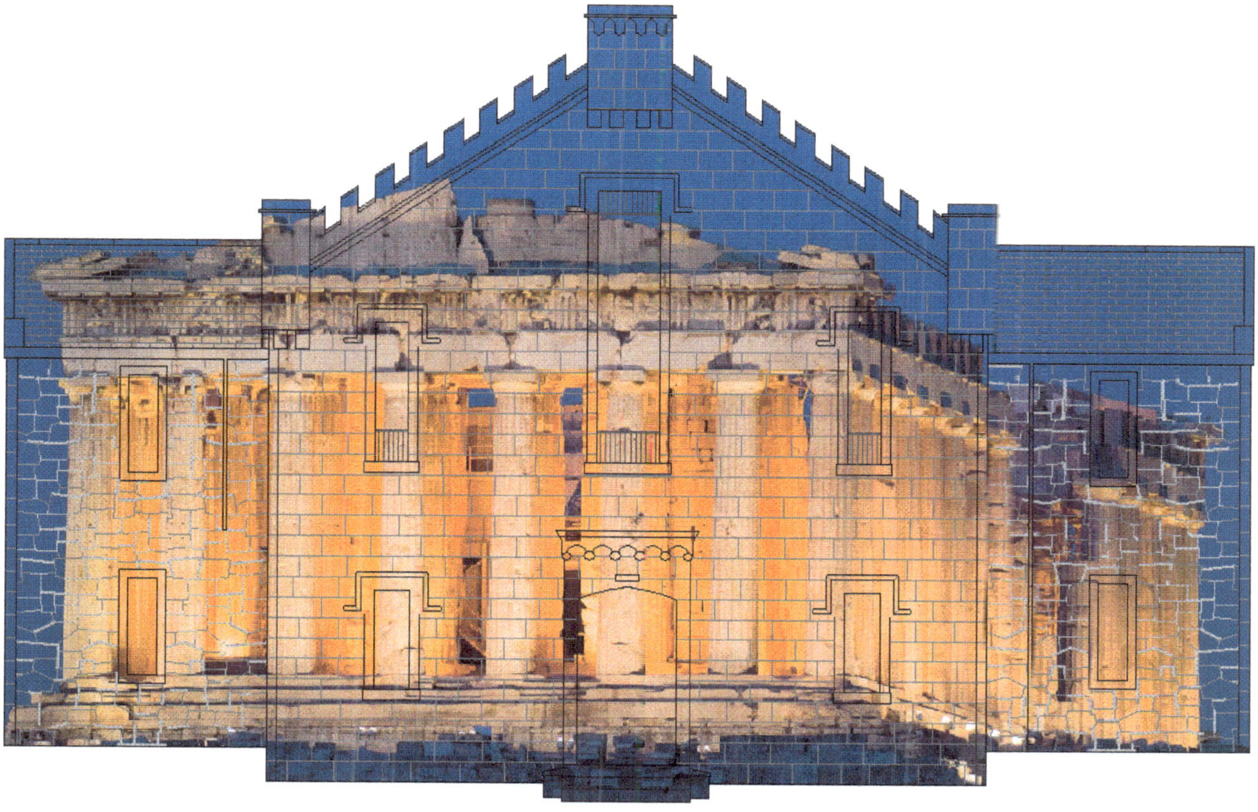

Hardgate Acropolis

The old Hardgate Hall, which was actually the Craigs Free Church built in 1781, is nowhere as old as the Athens Acropolis but if the supposed development of it doesn't get a move on it might just end up in as sad a state as the real Acropolis, and that's before the rebuilding that has been done since the Turks accidentally blew it up! Hopefully it will not cost as much, but who knows.

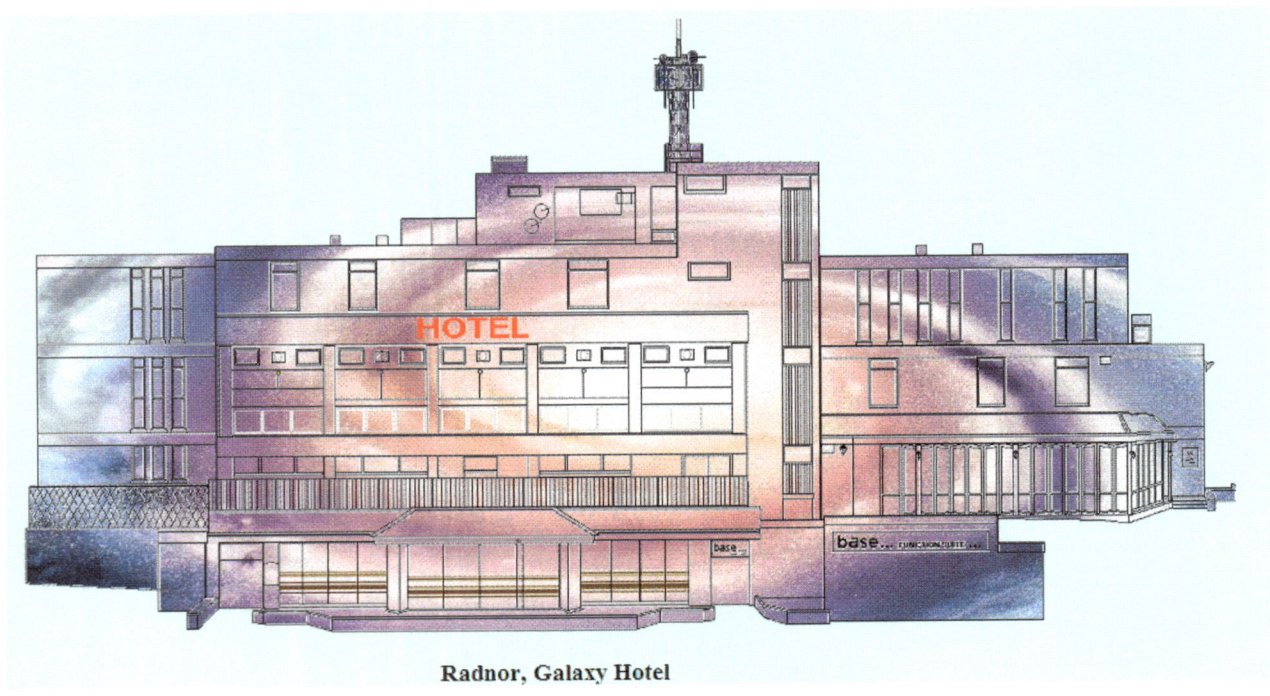

Radnor, Galaxy Hotel

Another I did using the Radnor Park Hotel now used as a canvas to show some galaxy or another. Don't ask me which as I am not really able to recognise one from another but this one was a nice fetching pink so there you are.

Maybe if I'm nice to the owners they will let me paint it like this, maybe even buy the paint for me? Well, it's better than letting it go to rot as it is doing now!

Just recently I found out that the Central Library was about to get a half million renovation job and an idea struck me. Right on the head probably which means I might just have concussion! No doubt it will mean shutting the place down for some time so why not just shift the books up to the Radnor, reopen the bar, and then we can all sit and have a pint and a read at the same time?

I'm also being selfish, as it means the library is nearer to me. Okay, it won't happen, but then why not open a bar in all the big libraries? Maybe then they would pay their way!

Okay, the bridge is familiar to most, especially if you have been to Venice and the mountains at the back are possibly recognisable to Alpine climbers, but the waterfall will likely only be recognised by keen travellers or South Africans. Of course though, the pub on the bridge will be known to the whole world as the famous Village Tavern in Duntocher!

If it's not, it's high time you all went there for a drink or two!

And by the way, I am not being paid a fortune by the owner to advertise- though I am open to offers!

Scenic Duntocher

I imagine the founding fathers of the Auld Kirk in Duntocher would turn in their graves if they saw the paint job I have given to the church, but rest easily! The scenery is from the Garden of the Gods in Colorado, so what's wrong with that?

Garden of the Gods?

Titanic Bridge

What has the bridge over the Forth & Clyde Canal at the shopping centre got to do with RMS Titanic? Well hopefully nothing before, but now there is link-this picture!

Some frames just demand a very high building inside them, not a picture with lots of foreground or background, but a framed piece of concrete steel and glass. My drawing of the Bilge pump demanded that so I had to again use some high flats, this time at the other end of the town in Yokerburn Terrace.

If it looks like some Sci –Fi robot marching in to crush Clydebank then maybe it is!

High Bilges!!!

Compressed Wimpey

Sixty odd years back Duntocher was almost trebled in size, area wise anyhow, by the might of the Wimpey building Co. Not everyone was pleased by that, not that I had views either way as I had not even heard of either Wimpey or Duntocher at the time!

Well now I've used the outline of an industrial refrigeration compressor to frame a typical Wimpey house it and if they want the size reduced, press the start button.

Not that I would expect the people who own this house to like that one wee bit!

So what's the Lucky Break Snooker Club, the Glenhead Tavern and me dressed up as a Roman soldier got to do with each other? Quite a lot really.

I've drank in the Glenhead, the Lucky Break, and Rome's airport and as of this moment feel like I've had a lucky break in my writing as my Kindle sales are doing well!

Just under a couple of thousand years back I suppose Roman soldiers were probably quite common at this spot pointing north to Caledonia which they hoped to conquer. They never did, got bogged down here in Duntocher and apart from a few forays north never got any further. I have to admit I do not think I would have made a good Roman soldier; I never was that keen on trudging through bogs and bracken, though I have to admit the odd Roman orgy might have been okay!

Lucky Break for the Romans

Vanguard

The last Battleship to be built in UK was HMS Vanguard, built down in John Browns, and I would have like to superimpose it against part of the yard buildings, but alas, nothing is left, so I've just slipped it onto a building probably as old, Davies Square in Duntocher. A long grey ship on a dull building. Not everything in Clydebank is colourful!

Kilbowie Road almost bisects Clydebank in a north to South direction and Kilbowie Hill dominates the town. Don't be fooled by those mountains at the back, they are somewhere in Canada! Now the battleship in the foreground is not in Canada, it's called the Alabama, and is in Mobile, Alabama. What's that got to do with Clydebank? Well that's my wife standing on the deck of it in her Titanic pose and she is in Clydebank, though no at that time, as we were both in Mobile visiting the ship. Impressive then, and there are a lot more ships etc now.

There were in all, eight USS Alabama's, a couple of the early one's built In UK, but none on the Clyde, though years ago if you had stood on Kilbowie hill the shipyards would have been visible easily and dominated by warships.

The Battleship Kilbowie!

Every now and again I find something around the town I had not noticed before, which is hardly surprising because the rock sitting below the flats at the top of Mountblow is on a side road. Why its there is another matter. I don't know, and like to think it has some significance, but if not, is a cheap, but effective, piece of sculpture and I'm all for the council not wasting money on Tombstones like those that run along Dumbarton Road.

Between a Rock and a Hard Place

Though these flats are not usually subjected to the near misses of others in the town which sit directly on the flight path into Glasgow airport or are at the top of a hill, I've stuck a plane up there anyway, just avoiding the buttes of Monument Valley in Arizona.

Get it? Monument, Tombstones, sculptures, rocks! No? Ah well, my picture and I can do what I want to, want to!

West end of California

Right, I'm off to the pub, and the favourites I've had is one of two usually. Unfortunately my one time favourite boozer was Clancy's in Long Beach and that's just too far away these days. So, I'll head up to the pub I've used above as a frame, The Village Tavern in Duntocher, better known as the West End.

Neither place can be said to have the greatest exterior but it's inside that counts and they both had heart, which is what makes a pub. If there was anything I would change about either I would plant Clancy's next to my house or maybe just provide the Village Tavern with some California weather!

Well enough of all this colour, it's giving me a headache, and so I'll finish with only a little colour and a lot of lines, my ugly mug mixed in with the outlines of a few buildings and a couple of pieces of machinery,

Pick them out if you can!

Just remember that some of those lines are genuinely on my face!

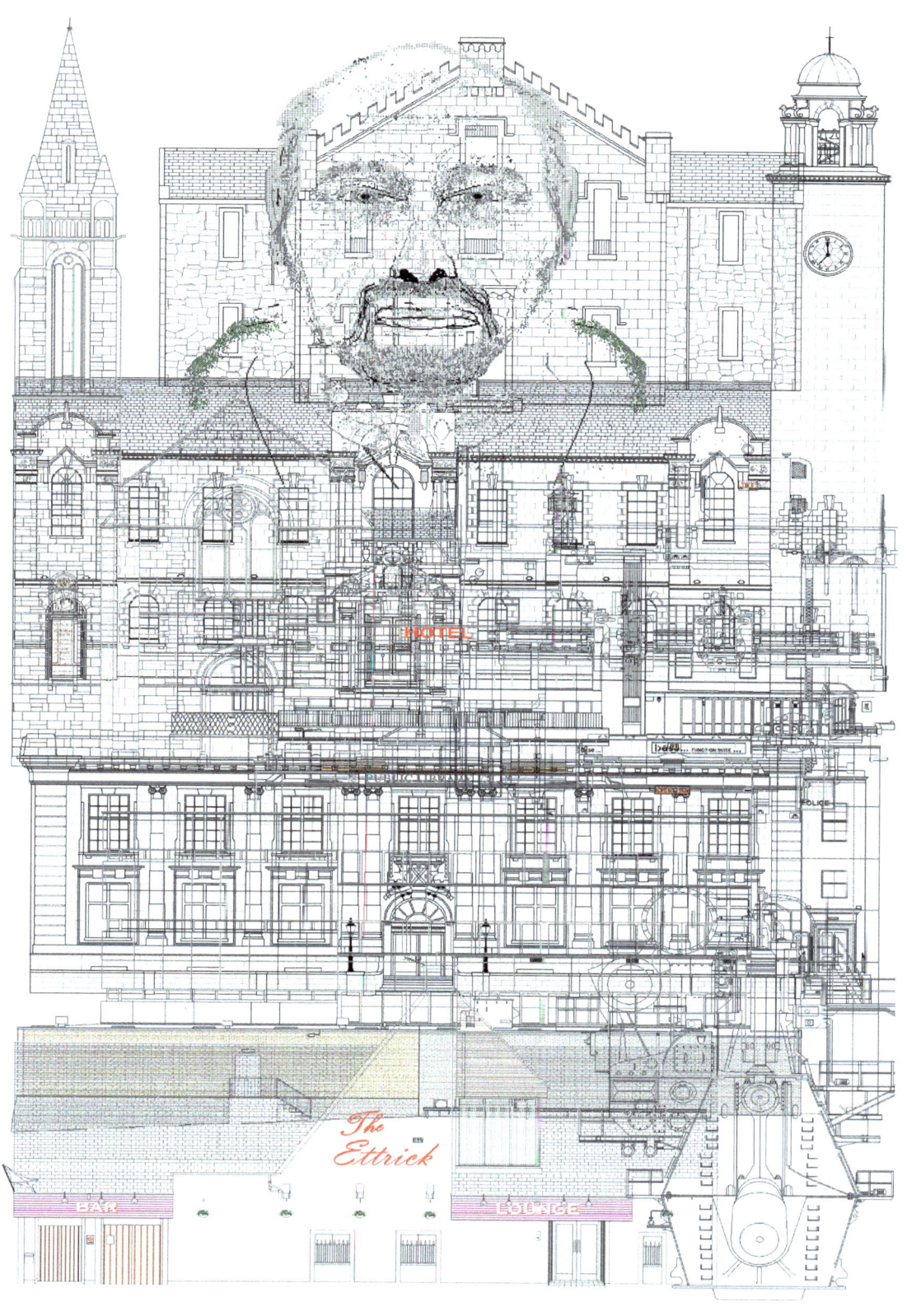

**Other books by Jack Kirk available on Amazon Books.
All fiction available on Kindle.**

Dark Immortal – Fiction -   Adventure and crime. 1st of Immortal series.

Red Immortal – Fiction -   Adventure and crime. 2nd of Immortal series.

Village of Fear - Fiction- Adventure & Crime- Set in Philadelphia present day.

A Flood of Spears- Fiction-Adventure with a magic touch. Set in a fictitious 11th century Britain with a difference. First of Fire Mountains series.

A Torrent of Ships- Fiction-Adventure with a magic touch. Set in a fictitious 11th century Britain with a difference. Second of Fire Mountains series. (2 books)

Defend or Die – Science Fiction- An alien invasion of Earth in the present day. 1st in Aakron Annihilation series (3 books)

Defy and Deny – Science Fiction- An alien invasion of Earth in the present day. 2nd in Aakron Annihilation series (3 books)

Attack and Annihilate - Science Fiction- An alien invasion of Earth in the present day. 3rd in Aakron Annihilation series (3 books)

A Basket of Life and Death- Fiction. Short stories. With a few Illustrations.

Imagination- Fiction. Poetry & Clipart-Illustrated.

Voyages 1- Fact- The author's life in the British Merchant Navy as an Engineer. Years 1968 to 1991. (2 books)

 Voyages 2- Fact- The author's life in the British Merchant Navy as an Engineer. Years 1991 to 2006. (2 books)

Digital Duntocher- Fact- An Illustrated view of the small Village of Duntocher, Scotland, showing typical and prominent buildings in and around it.

The Malevolent Machinery- Illustrated Humour-The authors take on the danger from machinery

Malky Machinery Colouring Book- Colouring book for Adults and children

The Bankie Booze Trail- Humorous illustrated guide to Clydebank pubs.

Kilbowie Church 2009

The End

www.ingramcontent.com/pod-product-compliance
Lightning Source LLC
Chambersburg PA
CBHW050819180526
45159CB00004B/1722